GUINNESS
BOOK OF Trivia
Records

GUINNESS
BOOK OF Trivia
Records

Illustrations by Bill Hinds

Sterling Publishing Co., Inc.   New York

Library of Congress Cataloging in Publication Data
Main entry under title:

Guinness book of trivia records.

"Based on the Guinness book of world records"—T.p
verso.
   Includes index.
   Summary: Cartoons illustrate a selection of outrageous facts from the Guinness Book of World Records,
including a man eating an eleven-foot tree and other
records involving animals, mechanical contrivances,
foods, and sports.
   1. Curiosities and wonders.   [1. Curiosities and
wonders]   I. Hinds, Bill, 1950–   ill.
AG243.G865   1985   031′.02   84-24130
ISBN 0-8069-0268-X
ISBN 0-8069-0269-8 (lib. bdg.)

First published in 1985 by Sterling Publishing Co., Inc.
Two Park Avenue, New York, N.Y. 10016
Text based on *Guinness Book of World Records* © 1984
by Guinness Superlatives Ltd.
Art by Bill Hinds © 1984 by Sterling Publishing Co., Inc.
Distributed in Canada by Oak Tree Press Ltd.
℅ Canadian Manda Group, P.O. Box 920, Station U
Toronto, Ontario, Canada M8Z 5P9
Manufactured in the United States of America

Contents

INTRODUCTION

The Guinness Book of World Records presents the most outrageous records in matter-of-fact reportage, sometimes with tongue-in-cheek. This gives Bill Hinds an opportunity to use his infectious sense of humor to satirize and humanize in cartoon form these straight statements of fact. In other words, he points up the zany with his art.

You see a young man eating an 11-foot tree as if he's enjoying the taste of the wood and is crazy to eat more. And that man on the wing of a plane, standing up in the breeze all the way across the Atlantic, seems to be quite sane, intent on doing something no one else has done.

Bill Hinds doesn't put down anyone, no matter how odd the record may seem. He accepts each record in good faith, but examines it with common sense. And his good common sense is what makes this book such fun. As you look through these pages, you'll see 500-plus cartoons that include more than humans—there are animals, places, mechanical contrivances, foods and entertainment feats, sports in particular. Take a look at the far-sighted eagle as Hinds sees him. Then there's the baseball player who had so little skill getting hits by swinging a bat that he became adept at getting hit by the pitcher. Either way he got to first base. How does Bill Hinds portray him? In a suit of armor, of course!

It's not easy to maintain your sanity in this crazy world. Does it make sense to break records? Does a man atop a 40-foot-high unicycle get a different view of the world as he rolls along than a driver of a car on the road below?

We think the answer is yes: every person in the Guinness Book feels he or she has done a worthwhile thing. They're all proud to be in it. Why? Because being in the book means they are No. 1 in their categories. And if Bill Hinds pokes some gentle fun at these top performers, it only reinforces the pleasure they get from being in the Book in the first place.

But humor fans and recordbreakers are not the only ones who will love this book. Trivia pursuers, those serious searchers, will find a whole barrelful of facts here—the kind of trivia they won't want to forget.

Have fun with these records—go to it—and don't complain if you wear out your chuckle muscle!

1 Stunts and Feats

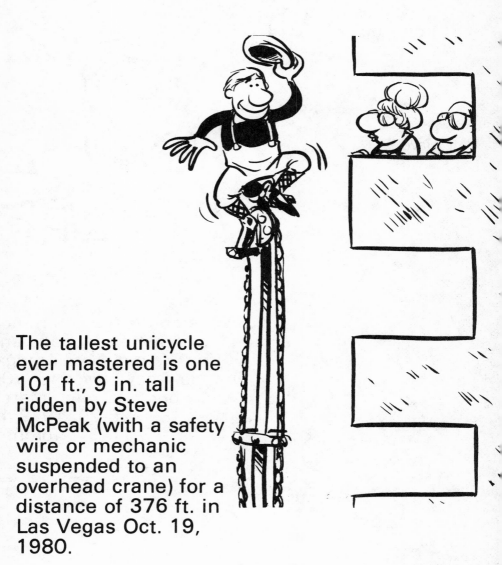

The tallest unicycle ever mastered is one 101 ft., 9 in. tall ridden by Steve McPeak (with a safety wire or mechanic suspended to an overhead crane) for a distance of 376 ft. in Las Vegas Oct. 19, 1980.

Mark Vinchesi set the record for maximum time aloft by keeping a Frisbee in the air for 15.2 seconds in Amherst, Mass., on Aug. 20, 1978.

The two-person frisbee marathon record is held by Ken McDade and Chris Train of Mississauga, Ontario. They played for 100 hours, 40 min., March 25-29, 1979, in Toronto.

Alan Bonopane threw a professional model Frisbee disc at a speed of 74 mph and his teammate Tom Selinske made a clean catch of the throw on Aug. 25, 1980, in San Marino, Calif.

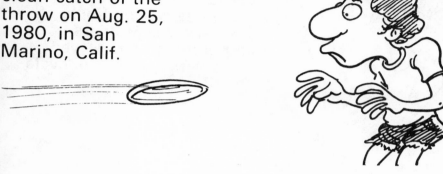

The best accepted ducks and drakes (stone-skipping) record is 24 skips (10 plinkers and 14 pitty-pats) by Warren Klope, 20, of Troy, Mich. with 14 thin, flat, 4-in. limestones, at the annual Mackinac Island, Mich. stone-skipping tournament July 5, 1975. This was equaled by John S. Kolar and Glenn Loy Jr. on July 4, 1977.

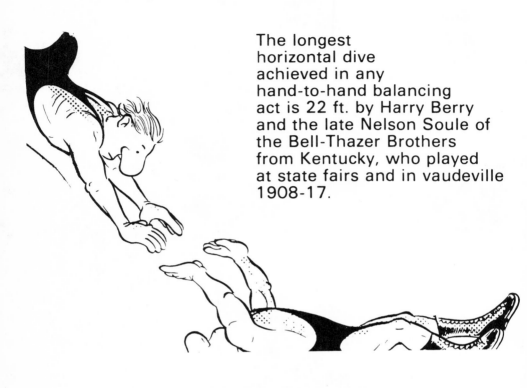

The longest
horizontal dive
achieved in any
hand-to-hand balancing
act is 22 ft. by Harry Berry
and the late Nelson Soule of
the Bell-Thazer Brothers
from Kentucky, who played
at state fairs and in vaudeville
1908-17.

David Steed of Tucson,
Ariz. stayed stationary
on a bicycle
without
support for 9
hours 15 min.
on Nov.
25, 1977.

Swami Maujgiri
Maharij stood up
continuously for 17
years, from 1955 to
November, 1973, while
performing the Tapasya
or penance in
Shahjahanpur, India. He
leaned against a
plank to sleep.

Bobby May can
juggle five
balls by
rebounding
them off a drum
on the floor
while he does
a headstand
on a table.

The lowest height for a flaming
bar under which a limbo dancer
has passed is 6⅛ in. off the
floor at Port of
Spain Pavilion,
Toronto, on
June 24, 1973,
by Marlene
Raymond, 15.

The record number of strands
of cotton threaded through a
No. 13 needle in two hours is
3,795 by Brenda Robinson
of Chippenham,
Wiltshire,
England, on
March 20,
1971.

Two kitchen hands, Harold Witcomb
and Gerald Harding, shelled 1,050
dozen eggs in a 7¼-hour shift at
Bowyers, Trowbridge, Wiltshire,
England Apr. 23, 1971. Both are
blind.

The longest recorded disco dancing
marathon is one of 371 hours
by John Sharples of Preston, England,
Jan. 18-Feb. 3, 1982.

Timothy
Roy
entered a
tree house in
Norwalk, Calif.,
on July 4, 1982,
and was still up there
a year later.

Paul Shirley, 21, of
Sydney, Australia,
made a piece of Life
Savers candy last in
his mouth for 4
hours 40 minutes
on Feb.
15, 1979,
before
the hole
broke up.

17

Henri La
Mothe (b.1904)
set a record for the
highest shallow dive by
diving 28 ft. into 12⅜
inches of water in a
child's wading pool
on Apr. 7, 1979 in
Northridge, Calif. for a
Guinness TV program.

The land divers of
Pentecost Island, New
Hebrides, dive from
70-foot-high platforms
with liana vines
attached to their
ankles. The resulting
jerk can transmit a
momentary force in
excess of 100 g.

The highest regularly
performed dive is that of
professional divers from
La Quebrada ("the break
in the rocks") at Acapulco,
Mexico, a height of 118
ft. The water is only
12 ft. deep.

The "strongest teeth in the world" belong to John "Hercules" Massis of Oostakker, Belgium, who at Evrey, France on March 19, 1977, raised a weight of 513⅝ pounds to a height of 6 inches from the ground with a bit in his teeth. Massis prevented a helicopter from taking off using only a mouth harness in Los Angeles April 7, 1979, for the "Guinness Spectacular" ABC-TV show.

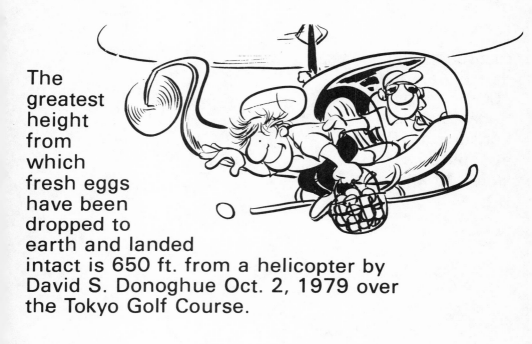

The greatest height from which fresh eggs have been dropped to earth and landed intact is 650 ft. from a helicopter by David S. Donoghue Oct. 2, 1979 over the Tokyo Golf Course.

Gerry O'Kane, 21, from Strath-clyde, Scotland, completed a 27-mile fresh egg and dessert spoon marathon in 5 hours 27 minutes on April 7, 1977.

21

The longest recorded belly dance was one of 100 hours by Sabra Starr of Lansdowne, Pa., at Teplitzki's Hotel, Atlantic City, N.J. July 4-8, 1977.

The most renowned of all escape artists has been Ehrich Weiss *alias* Harry Houdini (1874–1926), who pioneered underwater escapes from locked, roped and weighted containers while handcuffed and shackled with irons.

Mario Manzini, an escape artist from New York City, was suspended upside-down 20 feet above the ground securely tied in a Humane Restraint straitjacket and escaped within 8½ seconds on Aug. 8, 1979, on the "Guinness Game" TV show.

According to straitjacket manufacturers, an escapologist "skilled in the art of bone and muscle manipulation" could escape from a standard jacket in seconds. The fastest acknowledged claim is 1.68 seconds.

Lead climber Jean-Claude
Droyer of Paris, France,
and Pierre Puiseux of
Pau, France, climbed
up the outside of the
Eiffel Tower to a height
of 984 ft. in 2 hours 18
min. on July 21,
1980.

The endurance record for ferris wheel riding is 37 days by Rena Clark and Jeff Block at Frontier Village Amusement Park, San Jose, California, July 1—August 7, 1978.

The longest recorded push of a bed is 3,233 miles 1,150 yards in the case of a wheeled hospital bed by a team of nine employees of Bruntsfield Bedding Centre, Edinburgh, Scotland, June 21-July 26, 1979.

The greatest distance for paddling a hand-propelled bathtub in 24 hours is 55 miles 425 yds. by a team of 25 from Worcester Canoe Club, England Sept. 28-29, 1979.

The longest reported toy balloon flight is one of 10,000 miles approximately from Dobbs Ferry, N.Y., to Wagga Wagga, Australia.

The greatest distance covered in 24 hours in pushing a baby carriage is 345.25 miles by Runner's Factory in Los Gatos, Calif. with an all-star team of 57 California runners June 23-24, 1979.

GUINNESS Book of Trivia Records

The longest recorded ride in full armor is one of 167 miles from Edinburgh to Dumfries, Scotland, in 3 days (total riding time 28 hours 30 minutes) by Dick Brown, age 48, on June 13-15, 1979.

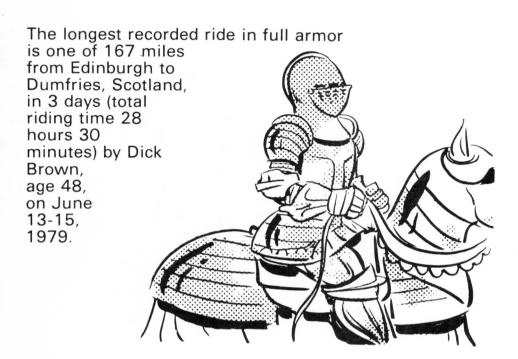

The record for carrying a brick (8 lbs. 15 oz.) in a nominated ungloved hand with the arm extended in an uncradled downward pincer grip is 45 miles by David and Kym Barger of Lamar, Mo., on May 21, 1977.

The endurance record for riding on a roller coaster is 368 hours by Jim King at the Miracle Strip Amusement Park, Panama City, Fla., June 22-July 7, 1980. He covered a distance of 10,425 miles.

Kevin St. Onge threw a standard playing card 185 feet at Henry Ford Community College, Dearborn, Mich., on June 12, 1979.

Norman Johnson of the Blackpool College of Art and Technology, England, sliced 12 inches of a 1½-inch-diameter cucumber into 20 slices to the inch in 24.2 seconds, on September 28, 1973.

Canal Jumping:
Douwe Bult
(Netherlands) leapt 43 ft.
8¾ in. across water by
swinging on a pole
to win the event on
the Japanese TV show
"Challenge the Guinness '80."

The record for the annual international 36-mile Nanaimo-to-Vancouver, British Columbia, bathtub race is 1 hour 29 minutes 40 seconds by Gary Deathbridge, 25 (Australia) July 30, 1978.

The longest recorded duration for balancing on one foot is 33 hours by V.S. Kumar Anandan of Colombo, Sri Lanka, May 15-17, 1980. The disengaged foot may not be rested on the standing foot nor may any sticks be used for support or balance, but 5-minute rest breaks are allowed after each hour.

The greatest recorded feat of coin balancing is the stacking of 170 Canadian coins on top of a Canadian Commemorative penny which was free-standing vertically on another coin by Bruce McConachy (b. 1963) of West Vancouver, British Columbia, on Aug. 24, 1979.

The official distance
record for barrel
jumping is 28 ft.,
8 in. over 17
barrels by
Kenneth Lebel
at Liberty, N.Y.
on Feb. 12, 1965.

Some 20¾
hamburgers and
buns were eaten in 30
minutes by Alan Peterson
at Longview,
Wash., on
Feb. 8,
1979.

GUINNESS Book of Trivia Records

The longest recorded conga line was a "snake" of 8,128 people in Sidmouth, Devon, England Aug. 25, 1978.

The longest piano-playing marathon has been one of 1,218 hours (50 days 18 hours) by David Scott May 7-June 27, 1982, at Wagga Wagga League's Football Club, Australia.

Jaromir Wagner (b. Czechoslovakia, 1941) became the first man
to fly the Atlantic standing on the
wing of an aircraft. He took off
from Aberdeen, Scotland, on
Sept. 28, 1980.

Hermann Görner (Germany) once raised 24 men weighing 4,123 lbs. on a plank with the soles of his feet, and also carried on his back a 1,444-lb. piano for a distance of 52½ ft. on June 3, 1921.

Lang Martin of Charlotte, N.C., succeeded on Feb. 9, 1980, in balancing seven new golf balls vertically without using any adhesive, beating his own record of six in 1977.

Alfonso Salvo of York, Pa.,
peeled 50 pounds of
onions (52 onions) in 5
min. 23 sec.
on Oct.
23, 1980.

The record duration for
continuous swinging is
185 hours by Mollie
Jackson at Mary-
mount College,
Tarrytown, N.Y.,
March 25-Apr.
1, 1979.

The longest recorded distance for driving on two wheels by a professional stuntman is 5.6 miles in a Chevrolet Chevette by Joie Chitwood Jr., on the Indianapolis Speedway, May 13, 1978.

The fastest time for window cleaning in the annual Ettore Challenge Cup in England has been 24 sec. plus ten ½-sec. smear penalties for 3 standard 40.94 x 45.39-in. office windows with an 11.8-in.-long squeegee and 15.83 pints of water.

STUNTS AND FEATS

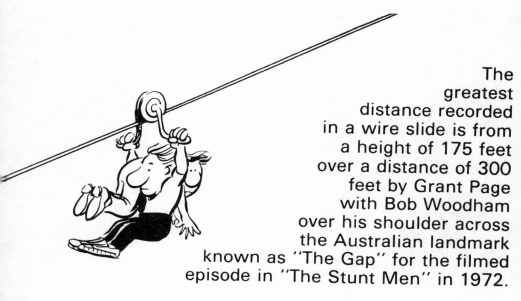

The greatest distance recorded in a wire slide is from a height of 175 feet over a distance of 300 feet by Grant Page with Bob Woodham over his shoulder across the Australian landmark known as "The Gap" for the filmed episode in "The Stunt Men" in 1972.

V. S. Kumar Anadan achieved 9,100 high kicks at Galle Face, Colombo, Sri Lanka, Dec. 31, 1980- Jan. 1, 1981. He took 6 hours 51 min., non-stop.

Dr. Allen Bussey completed 20,302 loops with a yo-yo in 3 hrs. on April 23, 1977 in Waco, Texas.

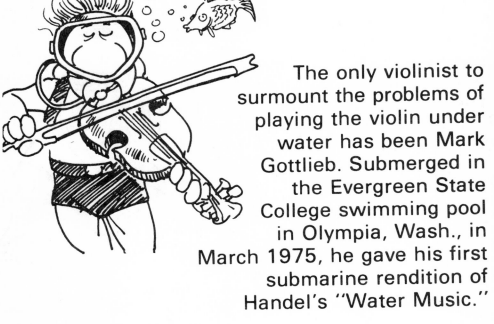

The only violinist to surmount the problems of playing the violin under water has been Mark Gottlieb. Submerged in the Evergreen State College swimming pool in Olympia, Wash., in March 1975, he gave his first submarine rendition of Handel's "Water Music."

The 3,200- ft.-wide
northwest face of Half Dome,
Yosemite, Calif., is 2,200 ft. high,
but nowhere departs more
than 7° from the vertical. It
was first climbed (Class VI) in
5 days in July 1957 by Royal
Robbins, Jerry Gallwas, and
Mike Sherrick.

The most
difficult tongue-
twister is deemed by Ken
Parkin of Teesside, England,
to be "The sixth sick sheik's
sixth sheep's sick" —
especially when
spoken
quickly.

The world's most difficult directory to tear in half is that for Houston, Tex., which runs to 2,889 pages for 939,640 listings. The easiest would be that for Farley, Mo.— 282 listings on 3 pages.

The women's non-stop talking record was set by Mrs. Mary E. Davis, who, Sept. 2-7, 1958, started talking at a radio station in Buffalo, N.Y., and did not draw breath until 110 hours, 30 min., 5 sec. later in Tulsa, Okla.

43

GUINNESS Book of Trivia Records

The longest tightrope walk by any funambulist was achieved by Henri Rochetain on a wire 3,790 yds. long slung across a gorge at Clermont-Ferrand, France, July 13, 1969. He required 3 hrs. 20 mins. to negotiate the crossing.

The fastest time up a 29.5-ft. coconut tree barefoot is 4.88 sec. by Fuatai Solo, 17, in Sukuna Park, Fiji, Aug. 22, 1980.

The greatest ascent on a high wire was achieved by Steve McPeak, when he walked 24,000 feet up a cable over Rio de Janeiro harbor in 1976.

The fastest time up a 40-ft. coconut tree barefoot is 8.4 sec. by Kini Marawai in Suva, Fiji, on Sept. 2, 1977.

Chester Cable
balanced a
130-lb. table
on his feet,
then twirled it
side over side as many
as 30 times in one
minute without stopping,
using only his legs.

The tightrope endurance record is
185 days by Henri Rochetain on a
wire 394 ft. long, 82 ft. above a
supermarket in St. Etienne, France,
March 28-Sept. 29, 1973. His ability
to sleep on the wire kept
doctors puzzled.

Edward Benjamin, known as Count Desmond (b. July 30, 1941, Binghamton, N.Y.), swallowed 13 23-inch-long blades to below his xiphisternum and injured himself in the process.

The greatest distance recorded for a slingshot is 1,434 feet 2 inches, using a 51-inch-long sling and a 2-ounce stone, by Lawrence L. Bray at Loa, Utah, on Aug. 21, 1981.

47

The 100-story record
for stair climbing was
set by Dennis W. Martz
in the Detroit Plaza Hotel,
Detroit, Mich., on June
26, 1978, at 11
minutes 23.8
seconds.

Even with a safety wire, very high stilts are extremely dangerous. John Russell, 26, of Appleton, Wis., working with the Ringling Bros. and Barnum & Bailey Circus, set a record for height by walking 34 steps on 33-ft.-high stilts at New York's Madison Square Garden on May 20, 1981, to beat his own record of 30 steps on 31-ft.-high stilts.

Because of their more optimal frequency, female screams register higher readings on decibel meters than male bellows. The highest scientifically measured emission has been one of 120 dBA on a Bruel & Kjaer Precision Sound Level Meter by Susan Birmingham at Hong Kong Island School March 6, 1982.

The women's record for non-stop piano playing is 133 hours by 280-lb. Marie Ashton, aged 40, in England, Aug. 18-23, 1958.

The most prolonged continuous shower bath on record is one of 336 hours by Arron Marshall of Rockingham Park, West Australia, July 29-Aug. 12, 1978.

The longest recorded survival alone on a raft is 133 days by Second Steward Poon Lim of the U.K. Merchant Navy, whose ship, the SS *Ben Lomond,* was torpedoed in the Atlantic 565 miles west of St. Paul's Rocks at 11:45 a.m. on Nov. 23, 1942. He was picked up by a Brazilian fishing boat April 5, 1943.

The greatest number of plates spun simultaneously is 72 by Shukuni Sasaki of Takamatsu, Japan, Nio Town Taiyo Exhibition, Kagawa, on July 16, 1981.

Jay Gwaltney ate an 11-ft.-tall birch sapling, including branches, leaves and the 4.7-in.-diameter trunk over a period of 89 hours to win $10,000 as first prize in a WKQX-Chicago radio station contest.

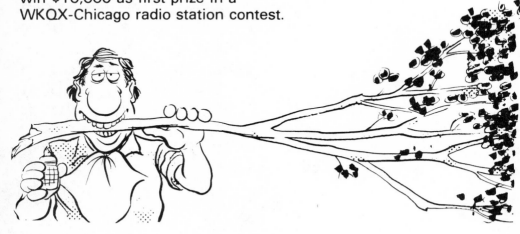

The record for projecting a melon seed under WCWSSA (World Championship Watermelon Seed Spitting Association) rules is 65 feet 4 inches by John Wilkinson in Luling, Texas, on June 28, 1980.

A beard of bees
estimated at not less
than 21,000
swarmed on the
chest and throat
of Don Cooke, of
Ohio, on
June 20,
1980.

Beverly Hills restaurateur Roger Bourban (b. May 10, 1948) ran a full marathon of 26 mi., 385 yards in full uniform in London, England, May 9, 1982, carrying a free-standing open bottle on a tray (gross weight 3 lb. 2 oz.) in 2 hours, 42 min., using the same hand the whole way.

The largest paper cup was a Dixie Cup, adorned with Guinness records. It was 6 ft. tall and 4¾ ft. across at the mouth and could hold 569 gallons of lemonade.

The longest
marathon merry-
go-round ride on
record is one of
312 hours 43
mins. by Gary
Mandau, Chris
Lyons and Dana
Dover in Portland,
Ore. Aug. 20-
Sept. 2, 1976.

Fourteen members of Phi Gamma
Delta fraternity at the University of
Seattle, Wash., leap-frogged 602
miles in 126 hours 46
minutes, March 20-25,
1981.

The greatest number of
lions mastered and fed
in a cage simultaneously by an unaided
lion-tamer was 40, by "Captain" Alfred
Schneider in 1925.

The duration record for walking-
on-hands is 871
miles by Johann
Hurlinger of
Austria, who, in 55
daily 10-hour stints,
averaged 1.58 mph
from Vienna to
Paris in 1900.

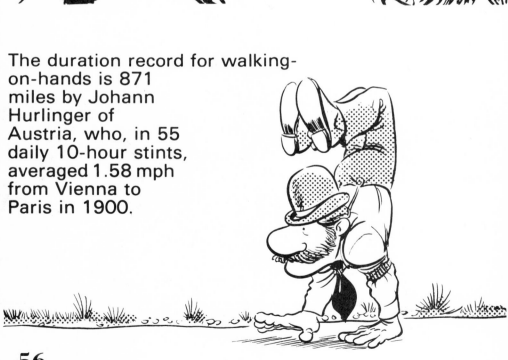

STUNTS AND FEATS

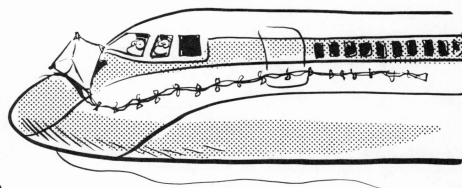

The
single
kite-flying altitude record is 22,500 ft. (minimum)
to 28,000 ft. (maximum) by Prof. Phillip R. Kunz
and Jay P. Kunz at Laramie, Wyo. Nov. 21, 1967.
Only rangefinder or radar verifications are
accepted by the American
Kitefliers' Association.

Thomas L. Gaddie rode 11,217.2
miles from Dallas, Texas, to Fairbanks,
Alaska, and back in 295
days, Feb. 12-Dec. 2,
1980, with seven
horses.

For a T.V. show, Shannon
Faucher, a 23-year-
old college student
from Los Angeles,
jumped from a flat
standing position
to a standing
position on top
of a refrigerator
55 inches high
to set a jumping
stunt record.

The fastest recorded time for a
100-yard three-legged race is
11.0 seconds by
Olympic medalists
Harry L. Hillman
and Lawson
Robertson in
Brooklyn,
New York,
on April 24,
1909.

The longest continuous voluntary crawl
(progression with one or the other knee in
unbroken contact with the ground) on
record is 26.5 miles by Rod Mahon and
Ken Mackenzie of Newtown Abbot,
England, on Jan. 18, 1982.

Joe Darby cleared a 12-foot billiard table lengthwise, taking off from a running start, using only a 4-inch-high solid wooden block, at Wolverhampton, England, Feb. 5, 1892.

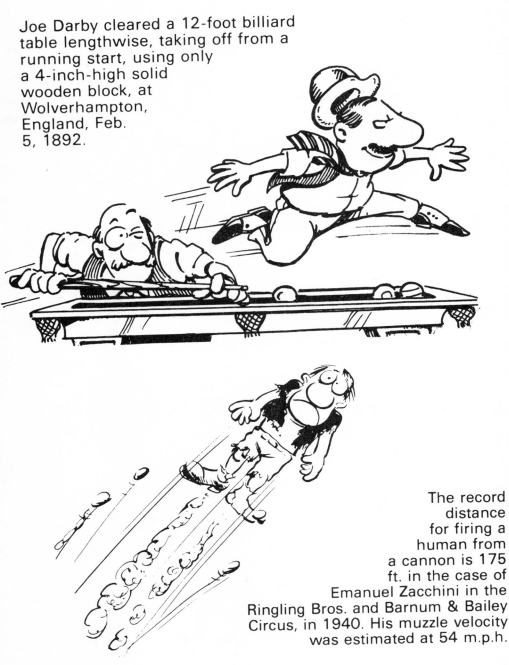

The record distance for firing a human from a cannon is 175 ft. in the case of Emanuel Zacchini in the Ringling Bros. and Barnum & Bailey Circus, in 1940. His muzzle velocity was estimated at 54 m.p.h.

STUNTS AND FEATS

The record for handshaking was set
by President Theodore
Roosevelt (1858-
1919), who
shook hands
with 8,513
people at a
New Year's Day
White House
presentation in
Washington, D.C.
Jan. 1, 1907.

The greatest reported achievement
in hair splitting has been that of the
former champion cyclist
and craftsman Alfred
West (b. London, Apr.
14, 1901) who split a
human hair 17 times
into 18 parts
on 8 occasions.

GUINNESS Book of Trivia Records

In 1968 it was
reported that Zolilio Diaz
(Spain) had rolled a
hoop 600 miles from
Mieres to Madrid
and back in
18 days.

The
longest
recorded distance
for catching a thrown grape in the
mouth is 319 ft. 8 in.
by Arden Chapman
of Pioneer, La.,
July 18, 1980.
The thrower was
Jerry "Pete" Mercer.

The only living man in the world to be struck by lightning 7 times is former Shenandoah Park Ranger Roy C. Sullivan, the human lightning-conductor of Virginia. He can offer no explanation for his magnetism.

Dean Moon of Santa Fe Springs, Calif., was due 1 cent from a miscalculation on a UPS shipment and the transportation company delivered a check for the full amount.

The most prolific hand-knitter has been Mrs. Gwen Matthewman of Featherstone, West Yorkshire, England, who in 1979 knitted 915 garments involving 11,012 ounces of wool.

Mrs. Barbara Jean Sonntag of Craig, Colo., crocheted 330 shells plus 5 stitches (equivalent to 4,412 stitches) in 30 minutes, at a rate of 147 stitches per minute, on Jan. 13, 1981.

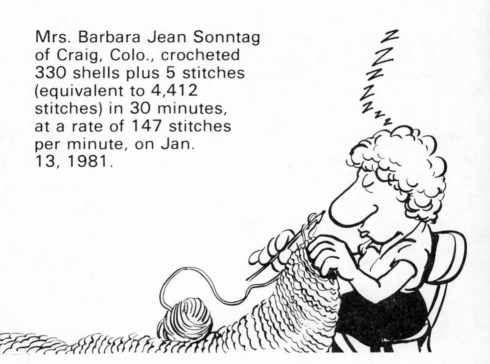

The longest recorded duration of a "rockathon" is 432 hours by Mrs. Maureen Weston of Peterborough, Cambridge, England, April 14-May 2, 1977.

For club swinging Bill Franks set a world record of 17,280 revolutions (4.8 per sec.) in 60 min. at Webb's Gymnasium, Newcastle, NSW, Australia Aug. 2, 1934. M. Dobrilla swung continuously for 144 hours at Cobar, NSW, Australia, finishing on Sept. 15, 1913.

The fastest *rate* ever measured for any tap dancer has been 1,440 taps per min. (24 per sec.) by Roy Castle on the BBC-TV *Record Breakers* program on Jan. 14, 1973.

STUNTS AND FEATS

The record number of
International Championships
is 10 by Jubiel Wickheim (of Shawnigan Lake,
BC, Canada) between 1956 and 1969. At Albany,
Ore., on July 4, 1956, Wickheim rolled on a
14-in. log against
Chuck Harris of
Kelso,
Wash., for
2 hours 40
min. before
losing.

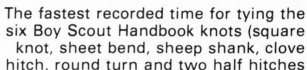

The fastest recorded time for tying the
six Boy Scout Handbook knots (square
knot, sheet bend, sheep shank, clove
hitch, round turn and two half hitches
and bowline) on
individual ropes is
8.1 sec. by
Clinton R. Bailey
Sr., 52, of Pacific
City, Ore., on
Apr. 13,
1977.

The duration record for non-stop lying on a bed of nails (sharp 6-inch nails 2 inches apart) is 102 hours 23½ minutes by the Rev. Ken Owen at the YMCA, Port Talbot, Wales, Sept. 29-Oct. 3, 1980.

V. Paratore and B. Galvin maintained a hammock in constant swinging motion for 192 hours in San Francisco in April, 1979.

Hugh Glass crawled 100 miles dragging a broken leg in 1823.

GUINNESS Book of Trivia Records

The largest dance ever
staged was that put on
by the Houston Livestock Show at the
Astro Hall, Houston, Tex., Feb. 8, 1969.
The attendance was 16,500, with
4,000 turned away.

The greatest recorded performance of
apple picking is 365½ U.S. bushels
picked in 8 hours by George Adrian,
32, of Indianapolis, on Sept. 23,
1980.

STUNTS AND FEATS

Mr. Lavor Taylor
(b. Feb. 27, 1896)
of Ephraim, Utah claims
to have sheared
513,000 sheep
to Feb. 1982.

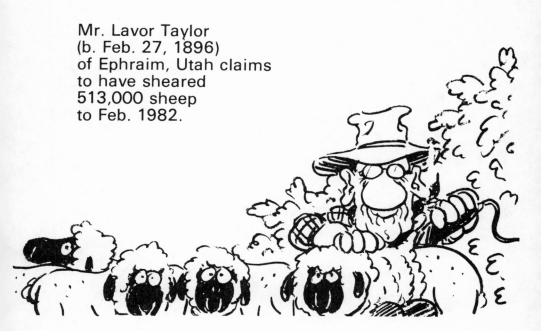

2   Entertainment

Morris Katz (b. 1932) of New York is the most prolific painter of saleable portraits in the world. His total sold, as of April, 1982, was 110,600.

GUINNESS Book of Trivia Records

The youngest person ever to accumulate $1 million dollars was the child film actor Jackie Coogan, co-star of "The Kid," made in 1920.

The most prolonged kissing marathon in cinematic history is one of 185 seconds by Regis Toomey and Jane Wyman in *You're In the Army Now,* released in 1940.

The largest loss incurred in a Broadway production was an estimated $2 million on *Frankenstein* which opened and closed Jan. 4, 1981.

The first actual golden disc was one sprayed by RCA Victor for presentation to Glenn Miller (1904-44) for his *Chattanooga Choo Choo* on Feb. 10, 1942.

GUINNESS Book of Trivia Records

Most Durable Actor: Richard Hearne (b. in Norwich, England, 1909) played a baby at the age of 6 weeks and performed continuously through childhood in circus, pantomime and musical comedy. On Christmas 1977, he was in *Cinderella* at the London Palladium.

The youngest recorded commercially published author is Dorothy Straight (b. May 25, 1958) of Washington, D.C., who wrote *How the World Began* in 1962, aged 4. It was published in Aug. 1964 by Pantheon Books.

The longest period of time for which a modern drawing has hung upside down in a public gallery unnoticed is 47 days. This occurred to *Le Bateau,* by Henri Matisse, in the Museum of Modern Art, New York City, between October 18 and December 4, 1961. In this time 116,000 people had passed through the gallery.

GUINNESS Book of Trivia Records

The world's largest permanent circus is Circus Circus, Las Vegas, Nevada, opened on October 18, 1968, at a cost of $15,000,000. It covers an area of 129,000 square feet.

The longest film ever released was * * * * by Andy Warhol, which lasted 24 hours. It proved a commercial failure, and was withdrawn and re-released in 90-minute form as *The Loves of Ondine.*

The most prolific television writer in the world is the Rt. Hon. Lord Willis, who in the period 1949-78 has created 23 series, 22 stage plays and 21 feature films. His total output since 1945 can be estimated at 15,000,000 words.

In one year, Parker Bros. prints more "money" — $18,500,000,000,000 — for its games than the total amount of real money printed in the entire world.

The unanimous choice for worst singer: Florence Jenkins (1868-1944), whose career culminated in 1944 with a sell-out concert at Carnegie Hall in New York.

John A. Wismont, Jr. (b. N.Y.C., Sept. 20, 1941), formerly of Disneyland, Anaheim, California, painted 45,423 watercolor paintings in his career (up to 1978) including 9,853 in 1976.

The longest non-scientific English words which can form anagrams are the 18-letter transpositions "conservationalists" and "conversationalists."

The world's largest art gallery is the Winter Palace and the neighboring Hermitage in Leningrad, U.S.S.R. One has to walk 15 miles to visit each of the 322 galleries, which house nearly 3,000,000 works of art and archeological remains.

GUINNESS Book of Trivia Records

The most overdue book taken out by a known borrower was a book on febrile diseases (London, 1805, by Dr. J. Currie) checked out in 1823 from the University of Cincinnati Medical Library and reported returned Dec. 7, 1968, by the borrower's great-grandson Richard Dodd. The fine was calculated as $2,264, but waived.

The largest book in the world is at U-Zoo & Co., Atlanta, Ga., measuring 16 feet x 14 feet, with 400 pages, made by Mead Paper Co. It is used as a stage when laid flat.

ENTERTAINMENT

The top-selling post card of all time was said to be a drawing by Donald McGill (1875-1962) with the caption: He: "How do you like Kipling?" She: "I don't know, you naughty boy, I've never Kippled." It sold about 6,000,000.

The champion writer of the goose-quill era was Jozef Kraszewski (1812-1887) of Poland, who produced more than 600 volumes of novels and historical works.

GUINNESS Book of Trivia Records

A bingo calling session of 265 hours, 1 min., was held at the Excess Sports and Social Club, Worthing, England, in Sept., 1981, with Alan Beech and Jeff McGee calling.

The oldest authoress was Mrs. Alice Pollock of Haslemere, Surrey, England, whose book *Portrait of My Victorian Youth* was published in March 1971 when she was 102 years 8 months.

The oldest existing commercial newspaper is the *Haarlems Dagblad/ Oprechte Haarlemsche Courant,* published in Haarlem, in the Netherlands. The *Courant* was first issued as the *Weeckelycke Courante van Europa* on January 8, 1656, and a copy of issue No. 1 survives.

The most massive single issue of a newspaper was *The New York Times* of Sunday, October 17, 1965. It comprised 15 sections with a total of 946 pages, including about 1,200,000 lines of advertising. Each copy weighed 7½ lbs. and sold for 50 cents locally.

Among classical composers the most rapid was Wolfgang Amadeus Mozart (1756-91) of Austria, who wrote *c.* 1,000 musical compositions, of which only 70 were published before he died, aged 35.

The oldest competitive ballroom dancer is Albert J. Sylvester (born November 24, 1889) of Corsham, Wiltshire, England, who on April 26, 1977, won the topmost amateur Alex Moor award for a 10-dance test with his partner, Paula Smith, in Bath, England.

The largest curtain ever built was the bright orange-red 4½-ton 185-ft.-high curtain suspended 1,350 ft. above and across the Rifle Gap, Grand Hogback, Colo., by the Bulgarian-born sculptor Christo, on Aug. 10, 1971. It blew apart in a 50-m.p.h. gust of wind 27 hours later. The total cost of displaying this work of art was $750,000.

GUINNESS Book of Trivia Records

The largest and presumably also
the loudest playable guitar in
the world is one 8 feet 10 inches tall,
weighing 80 lbs. built by The Harmony
Company of Chicago and completed in April,
1970. It carries a $15,000 price
tag, and is now on display at
the Guinness World Records
Exhibit Hall
in New
York
City.

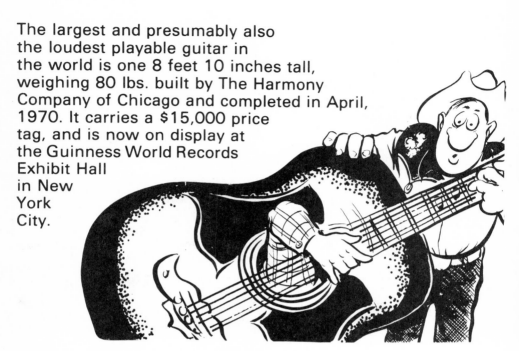

The earliest jazz record made was *Indiana* and
The Dark Town Strutters Ball, recorded for the
Columbia label in New York on or about Jan. 30,
1917, by the Original Dixieland Jazz Band,
led by Dominick (Nick) James La Rocca. This
was released
on May 31,
1917.

The greatest recorded number of curtain calls ever received by ballet dancers is 89 by Margot Fonteyn and Rudolf Nureyev, after a performance of "Swan Lake" at the Vienna Staatsoper, Austria, in October, 1964.

The individual continuous world record in ballroom dancing is 106 hours 5 minutes 10 seconds by Carlos Sandrini in Buenos Aires, Argentina, in September, 1955. Three girls worked shifts as his partner.

The world's first post cards were issued in Vienna on October 1, 1869. Pin-up girls came into vogue in 1914 having been pioneered in 1900 by Raphael Kirchner (1876-1917). The most expensive on record were ones made in ivory for an Indian prince which involved the killing of 60 elephants.

Stan Harper shows how to play the Hohner 48 Chord Harmonica, which, when separated, measures 4 feet long. It has 384 separate holes and can play in a total of 48 chords.

The record auction price for a thimble is $18,400 paid by the London dealer Winifred Williams at Christie's, London on Dec. 3, 1979, for a Meissen dentil-shaped porcelain piece of *c.* 1740.

The highest price ever paid for a portrait miniature is $172,500 by an anonymous buyer at a sale held by Sotheby's, London, Mar. 24, 1980, for a miniature of Jane Broughton, age 21, painted on vellum by Nicholas Hilliard (1547-1619) in 1574. The painted surface measures 1.65 in. in diameter.

3 Food

An edible house made
entirely of gingerbread
and icing (except for a
plywood floor) claims the record for
largest of its kind. Constructed in
December 1982 at the Amfac
Hotel at the Dallas/Ft. Worth
Regional Airport, it stands
13 feet high by 11 feet
deep.

The largest iced lollipop on a stick was one of 5,750 pounds, constructed for the Westside Assembly of God Church, Davenport, Iowa, Sept. 7, 1975.

The largest omelette ever made was one produced with 12,440 eggs in a pan measuring 30 feet by 10 feet, cooked by students at Conestoga College, Kitchener, Ontario, Canada, on June 29, 1979.

M. Lotito consumed a bicycle
in the form of stewed tires and
metal filings from March 17 to
April 2, 1977, in Evrey, France.

Some 12¾ doughnuts (weighing 51 ounces)
were eaten in 5 minutes 46 seconds by
James Wirth, and 13 (52 ounces) in 6
minutes 1.5 seconds by John Haight, both
at the Sheraton Inn, Canandaigua, N.Y.,
March 3, 1981.

GUINNESS Book of Trivia Records

One Imperial quart (1.2 U.S. quarts) of milk was consumed in 3.2 seconds by Peter Dowdeswell at Dudley Top Rank Club, West Midlands, England, on May 31, 1975.

Three pounds of shrimp were eaten in 4 minutes 8 seconds by Peter Dowdeswell at Earls Barton, England, on May 25, 1978.

Three pounds of
potatoes were eaten
in 1 minute 22 seconds by
Peter Dowdeswell
in Earls Barton,
England,
on Aug.
25,
1978.

Some 40 sandwiches (jam and
butter, 6 inches x 3¾ inches x ½
inch) were eaten in 17 minutes
53.9 seconds by Peter
Dowdeswell on Oct.
17, 1977, at the Donut Shop,
Reedley, Calif.

The largest mince pie ever baked was one of 2,260 lbs., measuring 20 feet by 5 feet, baked at Ashby-de-la-Zouch, Leicestershire, England, on Oct. 15, 1932.

The largest salami on record is one 29 feet 2¾ inches long with a circumference of 28 inches, weighing 734.13 pounds, made by Don Smallgoods for Australian Safeway Stores at Broadmeadow, Victoria, on April 23, 1982.

The largest cake ever assembled was the Baltimore City Bicentennial Cake of July 4, 1976, with ingredients weighing 69,860 pounds. An estimated 10,000 dozen eggs, 21,600 pounds of sugar, and a 415-pound pinch of salt were used.

Jim Ellis ate 3 lbs., 1 oz., of grapes in 34.6 seconds on May 30, 1976.

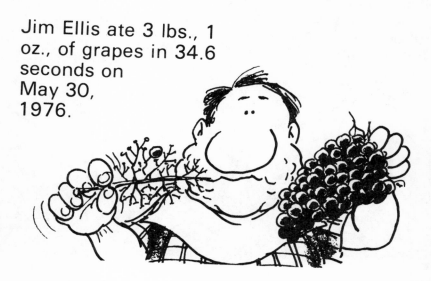

The longest one-piece loaf
ever baked was one of 1,256
feet 2¾ inches, created by Bruce Gajewski and
baked on the campus of Schenectady County
Community
College,
N.Y., in
an open
charcoal
oven
on
May
15,
1982.

The largest single dish is roasted camel,
prepared occasionally for Bedouin wedding
feasts. Cooked eggs are stuffed in fish, the
fish stuffed in cooked chicken, the chickens
stuffed into a roasted sheep carcass and
the sheep stuffed into a whole camel.

2,780 cold beans were eaten, one by one, with a cocktail stick, in 30 minutes by Karen Stevenson of Merseyside, England, April 4, 1981.

The record for eating lemons is held by Bobby Kempf of Roanoke, Va., who on May 2, 1979, ate 12 quarters (3 lemons, including skin and seeds) in 15.3 seconds.

GUINNESS Book of Trivia Records

A buffet table 2,692 feet 5 inches long with 20,000 dishes was set up by a hotelier in Marienheide, West Germany to feed 10,000 people attending a charitable fundraising outdoor event on April 22, 1978.

The greatest number of barrels of potatoes picked in a 9½-hour day is 235 by Walter Sirois (b. 1917) of Caribou Maine, on September 30, 1950.

Linda Kuerth, 21, ate 23 2-ounce frankfurters in 3 minutes, 10 seconds, at Veterans Stadium, Philadelphia, on July 12, 1977.

The record for eating 30 2-oz. bags of potato chips was set by Paul Tulley in Australia in May, 1969. He performed the feat in 24 minutes, 33.6 seconds, without a drink.

The highest claim for the number of yolks in a chicken's egg is 9 reported by Mrs. Diane Hainsworth of Hainsworth Poultry Farms, Mt. Morris, N.Y., in July 1971 and also from a hen in Kirghizia, U.S.S.R. in Aug. 1977.

The hottest of all spices is the capsicum hot pepper known as Tabasco, first reported in 1868 by Edmund McIlhenny on Avery Island, Louisiana.

Dr. Ronald L. Alkana ate 17 bananas on December 7, 1973 at the University of California, Irvine.

The record for chicken eating is held by "Bozo" Miller, who ate 27 chickens at one sitting at Trader Vic's, San Francisco in 1963.

GUINNESS Book of Trivia Records

The greatest meat eaters in the world are the people of the United States, with an average consumption of 10.89 ounces per person per day in 1977.

The largest kitchen ever set up was the Indian government field kitchen set up in April, 1973, at Ahmadnagar, Maharashtra, in a famine area, which daily provided 1,200,000 subsistence meals.

The record for eating
meat is held by Johann
Ketzler, Munich, Germany, who in 1880
consumed a whole roast ox in 42 days.

On March 9,
1978, Pat
Donahue ate 91 pickled
onions (30 oz.) in 1
min. 8 sec. at Victoria,
B.C., Canada.

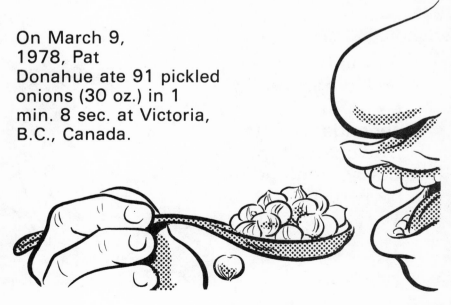

Ninety-six 1-ounce
sausages were eaten
in 6 minutes by
Steve Meltzer of
Brooklyn, N.Y., on
Oct. 14, 1974.

Fourteen hard-
boiled eggs were
eaten in 58
seconds by Peter
Dowdeswell in
Corby, England,
on Feb. 18,
1977.

The most monumental barbecue
has been one for 19,000 people
who consumed 46,000 barbecued
chicken halves at Iolani
School, Honolulu, Hawaii,
on Jan. 31, 1981.

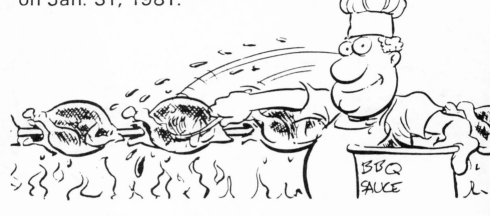

Residents of Belgium,
England and Switzerland
are said to be the
greatest consumers
of chocolate at
approximately 15½
pounds per year.

The largest pizza ever baked was one measuring 80 ft., 1 in. in diameter, 5,037 sq. ft. in area, and 18,664 lb. in weight at the Oma Pizza Restaurant, Glens Falls, N.Y., owned by Lorenzo Amato, on Oct. 8, 1978. It was cut into 60,318 slices.

4 Animals and Plants

On Feb. 28, 1980 a
female cat climbed 70
feet up the sheer outside
wall of a 5-story
apartment house in
Bradford, Yorkshire,
England, and took refuge
in a roof space. She had
been frightened by a dog.

The greatest mouser on record was a tabby named "Mickey," owned by Shepherd & Sons Ltd. of Lancashire, England, which killed more than 22,000 mice during 23 years.

In 1923 a collie named "Bobbie," lost by his owners while they were on vacation in Indiana, turned up at the family home in Silverton, Oregon, 6 months later, after having covered a distance of close to 2,000 miles.

The largest member
of the cat family
(Felidae) is the long-furred
Siberian tiger *(Panthera
tigris altaica),* also
known as the Amur
or Manchurian
tiger.

The greatest load
shifted by a dog was
6,400½ pounds of railroad steel pulled
by a 176-pound St. Bernard at Bothell,
Wash., July 21, 1978.

The largest litter ever recorded was one of 19 kittens (4 stillborn) delivered by Caesarean section to "Tarawood Antigone," a 4-year-old brown Burmese, on Aug. 7, 1970. Her owner, Mrs. Valerie Gane of Kingham, Oxfordshire, England, reported that the litter was the result of mismating with a half-Siamese.

The longest recorded canine long jump was one of 30 ft. by a greyhound named "Bang," made in jumping a gate in coursing a hare at Brecon Lodge, Gloucestershire, England, in 1849.

On July 17, 1981
"Young Sabre," a
German shepherd,
handled by Corporal
David Smith, beat
his own record
when he scaled an
11-ft.-8-in. wall at
RAF Newton,
Nottinghamshire,
England.

The fastest breed of dog (excluding the greyhound and possibly the whippet) is the saluki, also called the Arabian gazelle hound or Persian greyhound. Speeds up to 43 m.p.h. have been claimed.

The world's top police dog is "Trep" of Miami, Florida, who has sniffed out $63,000,000 worth of narcotics. In a school demonstration looking for 10 hidden packets, Trep once found 11.

116

The heaviest breed of chicken is one called the white sully, developed in West Point, Calif. One monstrous rooster named "Weirdo" reportedly weighed 22 lb. and was so ferocious he crippled a dog and killed two cats.

The largest chicken ranch is the 345-acre "Egg City," in Moorpark, Calif., established by Julius Goldman in 1961. Some 2,220,000 eggs are laid daily by 3 million hens.

GUINNESS Book of Trivia Records

The turkey farm of Bernard Matthews Ltd., centered at Great Witchingham, Norfolk, England, has 700 workers tending 4,000,000 turkeys.

The highest authenticated rate of egg-laying is by a white leghorn chicken hen at the College of Agriculture, University of Missouri, with 371 eggs in 364 days in an official test, conducted by Professor Harold V. Biellier, ending on Aug. 29, 1979.

The record distance flown by a chicken is 310 ft., 6 in., by *"Shorisha"* (means champion) owned by Morimitzu Neura at Hammatzu, Japan Mar. 8, 1981.

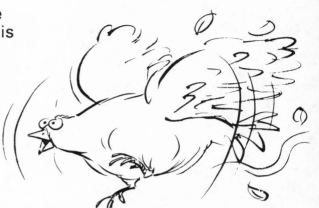

The highest recorded price paid for a pigeon is approximately $48,000 by a Japanese fancier for *De Wittslager* to Georges Desender (Belgium) in October, 1978.

The greatest reliable age
recorded for a horse is 62
years in the case of "Old Billy" (foaled 1760),
believed to be a cross between a Cleveland and an
Eastern blood, who was bred by Edward Robinson
of Wild Grave Farm in Woolston, Lancashire,
England.

The smallest breed of horse is the Falabella,
bred by Julio Falabella, developed over a
period of 45 years by crossing and recrossing
a small group of undersized English
thoroughbreds with
Shetland ponies.
Adult specimens
range from 15-30
in. at the
shoulder and
weigh 40-80
lb.

The longest-lived domesticated bird is the domestic goose, which normally lives about 25 years. A gander named "George," owned by Mrs. Florence Hull of Lancashire, England, died on Dec. 16, 1976, aged 49 years 8 months.

The largest living bird is the North African ostrich. Male examples have been recorded up to 9 feet in height and 345 pounds in weight.

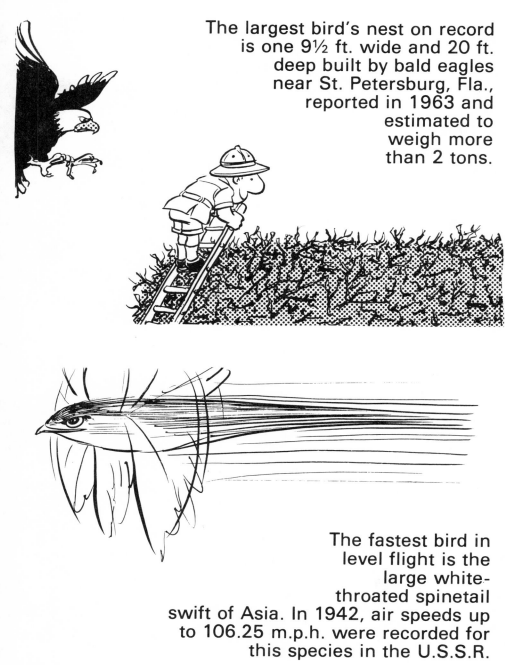

The largest bird's nest on record is one 9½ ft. wide and 20 ft. deep built by bald eagles near St. Petersburg, Fla., reported in 1963 and estimated to weigh more than 2 tons.

The fastest bird in level flight is the large white-throated spinetail swift of Asia. In 1942, air speeds up to 106.25 m.p.h. were recorded for this species in the U.S.S.R.

The greatest distance covered by a ringed bird during migration is 12,000 miles by an Arctic tern, which was banded as a nestling July 5, 1955, on the White Sea coast of the U.S.S.R., and was captured alive by a fisherman in Western Australia, May 16, 1956.

The smallest bird in the world is Helena's hummingbird. An average male adult has a wing span of 3 inches and weighs only 2 grams. It has an overall length of 2.28 inches, the bill and tail accounting for about 1.7 inches.

The heaviest hog recorded was the Poland-China hog "Big Bill" of 2,552 lb. measuring 9 ft. long with a belly on the ground, owned by Burford Butler of Jackson, Tenn., and chloroformed in 1933. He was mounted and displayed by the Wells family in Jackson, Tenn. until 1946.

The highest recorded catch of fish was 72,434,000 tons in 1973. Peru had the largest ever national haul with 13,406,000 tons in 1970, comprising mostly anchoveta.

Under
favorable
conditions
a golden
eagle can detect
an 18-inch long
hare at a range of
2,150 yards
(possibly even 2
miles).

The most powerful electric fish
is the electric eel, which is
found in the rivers of
Brazil, Colombia,
Venezuela and Peru.
An average-sized
specimen can
discharge 400 volts at
1 ampere, but
measurements up
to 650 volts have
been recorded.

The fastest swimmer is the Gentoo
penguin. In Jan., 1913 a small group
was timed at 22.3 m.p.h. underwater
near the Bay of Isles, South Georgia,
Falkland Islands, South Atlantic. This
is a respectable flying speed for some
birds.

126

The largest known invertebrate is the Atlantic giant squid *Architeuthis dux.* on Nov. 2, 1878, a specimen measuring 55 feet in total length was killed after it ran aground in Thimble Tickle Bay, Newfoundland, Canada. It weighed an estimated 4,400 pounds.

The fastest of all land animals over a short distance is the cheetah or hunting leopard *(Acinonyx jubatus)* of the open plains of East Africa, Iran, Turkmenia and Afghanistan, with a probable maximum speed of 60 to 63 mph over level ground.

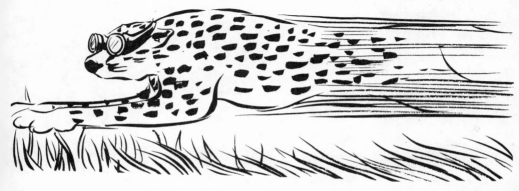

Perhaps the lowest ever price for
livestock was at a sale at Kuruman,
Cape Province, South Africa in
1934 where donkeys
were sold for less
than 4¢ each.

The sperm whale has
the heaviest brain of all
living animals. The brain
of a 49-foot-long bull
processed aboard
a Japanese factory
ship on December
11, 1949, weighed
20.24 lbs.

The largest concentration of wild mammals found living anywhere in the world today is that of the Brazilian free-tailed bat *(Tadarida brasiliensis)* in Bracken Cave, San Antonio, Texas, where up to 20 million animals assemble after migration.

The greatest irrefutable age reported for a primate (excluding humans) is *c.* 59 years in the case of a male orangutan named "Guas," who was received by the Philadelphia Zoo May 1, 1931, when he was at least 13 years old, and died Feb. 9, 1977.

The heaviest gorilla living in captivity today is a western lowland male called "Zaak," who was received at the Kobe Oji Zoo, Japan, in Dec. 1962. He tipped the scales at 628 lb. in June 1976, but has not been weighed since.

The slowest moving land mammal is the three-toed sloth of tropical America. The average ground speed is 6-8 ft. per min. (0.068 to 0.098 mph), but in the trees it can "accelerate" to 15 ft. per min. (0.170 mph).

The smallest monkey is the pygmy marmoset *(Cebuella pygmaea)* of the Upper Amazon Basin.

The Himalayan ibex escapes from hunters by leaping criss-cross down sheer cliffs, momentarily touching its hoofs down on rocky ledges.

The most elusive of all spiders are the rare trapdoor spiders of the genus *Liphistius,* which are found in Southeast Asia.

The centipede with the greatest number of legs is *Himantarum gabrielis* of southern Europe which has 171-177 pairs when adult.

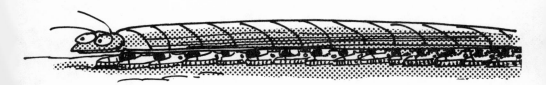

The largest known spiders are the
exceptionally bulky theraphosid
spiders of Brazil, which have been
credited with leg spans in excess
of 10 in. One female collected at
Manaos, Brazil, in 1945 measured
9½ in. across the legs.

The largest rodent is
the capybara, which
is found in tropical South America.
Mature specimens have a head and
body length of 3¼-4½ ft. and weigh
up to 174 lb.

"Dixie" owned by A. Newton of
Sheffield, Yorkshire, England, is the
oldest mouse on record, having died
on April 25, 1981,
aged
6½
yrs.

135

The longest animal ever recorded is the ribbon worm *Lineus longissimus,* also known as the "bootlace worm," which is found in the shallow coastal waters of the North Sea. In 1864 a specimen measuring more than 180 feet was washed ashore at St. Andrews, Fifeshire, Scotland, after a storm.

The largest reptile in the world is the estuarine or salt-water crocodile of Southeast Asia, northern Australia, New Guinea, the Malay Archipelago and the Solomon Islands. Adult males average 14-16 ft. in length and scale 900-1,150 lb.

The smallest known reptile is believed to be a tiny gecko found only on the island of Virgin Gorda, one of the British Virgin Islands. It is known only from 15 specimens found between Aug. 10 and 16, 1964. The three largest females measured 0.71 inch from snout to vent, with a tail of approximately the same length.

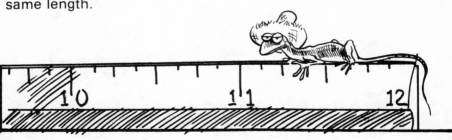

GUINNESS Book of Trivia Records

The longest of all snakes is the reticulated python of Southeast Asia, Indonesia and the Philippines, which regularly exceeds 20 ft. In 1912 a specimen measuring exactly 32 ft. 9½ in. was shot near a mining camp on the north coast of Celebes in the Malay archipelago.

The most intransigent weed is the mat-forming water weed *Salvinia auriculata,* found in Africa. It was detected on the filling of Kariba Lake, in May 1959 and within 11 months had choked an area of 77 sq. mi., rising by 1963 to 387 sq. mi.

The yellowish-olive death cup
(Amanita phalloides) is regarded
as the world's most poisonous
fungus. From 6 to 15 hours
after tasting, the effects are
vomiting, delirium, collapse
and death.

The mottled orange-brown and
white parasitic stinking corpse
lily has the largest of all blooms. These attach
themselves to the cissus vines of the jungle in
southeast Asia. They measure up to 3 ft.
across and ¾ in. thick, and attain a
weight of 15 lb.

ANIMALS AND PLANTS

The tallest known tree is the coast redwood. The tallest example measures 367.8 feet, and is located in Redwood Creek Grove, Humboldt County, Calif.

The heaviest of all woods is black ironwood, also called South African ironwood, with a specific gravity of up to 1.49, and weighing up to 93 lb. per cu. ft.

An apple weighing 3 lb. 1 oz. was reported by V. Loveridge of Ross-on-Wye, England in 1965.

The world's largest blossoming plant is the giant Chinese wisteria at Sierra Madre, California. It was planted in 1892 and now has branches 500 feet long. It covers nearly an acre, weighs 252 tons and has an estimated 1,500,000 blossoms during its blossoming period of five weeks.

The tallest cut Christmas tree was a 221-ft. Douglas fir erected at Northgate Shopping Center, Seattle, Wash., in Dec., 1950.

5   Things and Places

The longest stairs are the service staircase for the Niesenbahn funicular which rises to 7,759 ft. near Spiez, Switzerland. It has 11,674 steps and a banister. The T'ai Chan Temple stairs of 6,600 stone-cut steps in the Shantung Mts., China, ascend 4,700 ft. in 5 miles.

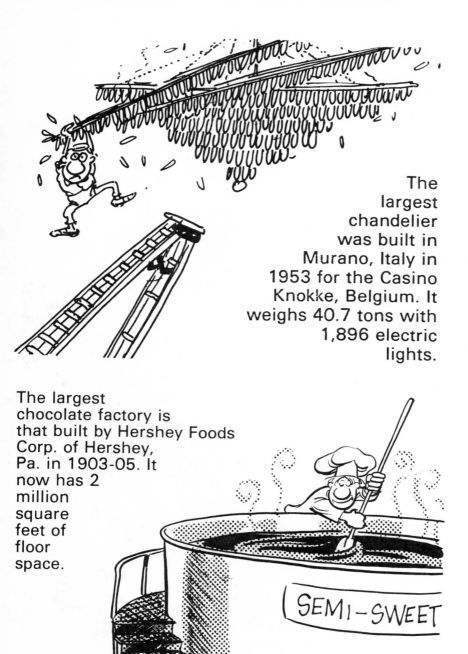

The
largest
chandelier
was built in
Murano, Italy in
1953 for the Casino
Knokke, Belgium. It
weighs 40.7 tons with
1,896 electric
lights.

The largest
chocolate factory is
that built by Hershey Foods
Corp. of Hershey,
Pa. in 1903-05. It
now has 2
million
square
feet of
floor
space.

SEMI-SWEET

146

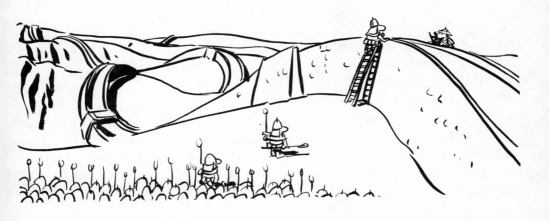

The Great Wall of China, completed during the Ch'in dynasty (246-210 B.C.), has a main-line length of 2,150 miles with a further 1,780 miles of branches and spurs, with a height of from 15 to 39 ft. and up to 32 ft. thick.

The highest recorded
mileage for a car was
1,184,880 authenticated miles by
August 1978 for a 1957 Mercedes
180D owned by Robert
O'Reilly of Olympia,
Wash. Its
subsequent
fate is
unknown.

The cheapest car of all-time was the
1922 Red Bug Buckboard, built by
Briggs and Stratton Co. of Milwaukee,
Wis. listed at $150-$125. It had a 62-
in. wheel base and weighed
245 lb. The early models of
the King Midget cars were
sold in kit form for self-
assembly for as little
as $100 as
late as
1948.

The longest tow on record
was one of 4,759 miles from
Halifax, Nova Scotia to Canada's Pacific coast,
when Frank J. Elliott and George A. Scott of
Amherst, Nova Scotia,
persuaded 168 passing
motorists in 89 days to
tow their Model T Ford
(in fact, engineless) to
win a $1,000
bet on Oct. 15,
1927.

Charles Creighton (1908-70) and James Hargis
of Maplewood, Mo., drove their Ford Model A
1929 roadster in reverse from New York to Los
Angeles (3,340 miles), July 26-Aug. 13, 1930,
without stopping the engine
once. They arrived back
in New York on Sept. 5,
again in reverse, thus
completing 7,180
miles in 42
days.

150

THINGS AND PLACES

The skid marks made by the jet-powered *Spirit of America,* driven by Craig Breedlove, after the car went out of control at Bonneville Salt Flats, Utah, on October 15, 1964, were nearly 6 miles long.

The world's first auto license plates were probably introduced by the Parisian police in France in 1893.

The most powerful wrecker is the Vance Corp 28-ton 30-foot-long Monster No. 2 stationed at Hammond, Ind. It can lift in excess of 179 tons on its short boom.

The largest tires are manufactured in Topeka, Kans. by the Goodyear Co. for giant dump trucks. They are 11 ft. 6 in. in diameter, weigh 12,500 lb. and cost more than $50,000.

The largest military
catapults, or onagers,
were capable of
throwing a
missile weighing
60 lb. a
distance of
500 yd.

A classic ordinary
bicycle with a 64-inch-
diameter front
wheel and a 20-
inch diameter
back wheel was
built *c.* 1886
by the Pope
Manufacturing
Co. of
Massachusetts.

The longest true tandem bicycle ever built is one of 66 ft. 11 in., for 35 riders, built by the Pedaalstompers Westmalle of Belgium. The machine weighs 2,425 lbs.

The longest time a solo motorcycle has been kept in continuous motion is 500 hours, by Owen Fitzgerald, Richard Kennett and Don Mitchell, in Western Australia, on July 10-31, 1977. They covered 8,432 miles.

From March 28 to
April 1, 1959, a
Ransome *Matador* motorized mower
was driven for 99
hours non-stop
over 375 miles
from Edinburgh
to London.

The lightest mechanically
powered airplane to have
flown by early 1981 was the solar-powered
Solar Challenger designed by a team led by
Dr. Paul MacCready. It had an empty
weight of 130 lb. and a
takeoff weight of 275.5 lb.,
which included its 99 lb.
pilot, Janice
Brown and
her parachute.

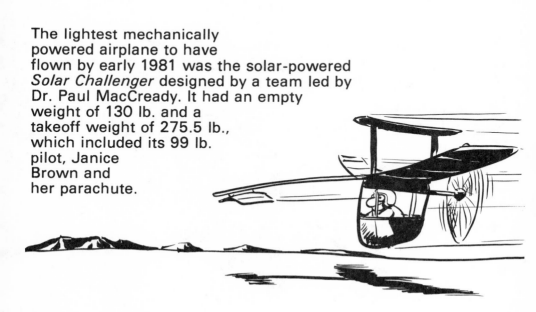

156

THINGS AND PLACES

The widest gang mower on record is the 5.6-ton 60-foot-wide 27-unit Big Green Machine, used by the sod farmer Jay Edgar Frick of Monroe, Ohio. It mows an acre in 60 seconds.

The fastest crossing of the Pacific Ocean by ship (4,840 nautical miles) was 6 days 1 hour 27 minutes by the containership *Sea-Land Commerce* from Yokohama, Japan, to Long Beach, Calif., in 1973, at an average speed of 33.27 knots (38.31 m.p.h.).

The only circumnavigation of the world by an amphibious vehicle was achieved by Ben Carlin (Australia) (d. March 7, 1981) in an amphibious jeep "Half-Safe." He completed the last leg of the Atlantic crossing (the English Channel) on Aug. 24, 1951. He arrived back in Montreal, Canada on May 8, 1958 having completed a circumnavigation of 39,000 miles over land and 9,600 miles by sea and river.

The longest fence is the dingo-proof fence enclosing the main sheep areas of Queensland, Australia. The wire fence is 6 ft. high, goes 1 ft. underground, and stretches for 3,437 miles, more than the distance from Seattle to N.Y.

The longest vehicle ever built is the Arctic Snow Train now owned by the world-famous wire-walker Steve McPeak. This 54-wheeled 572-foot-long vehicle was built by R.G. Le Tourneau Inc. of Longview, Texas for the U.S. Army. Its gross train weight is 400 tons with a top speed of 20 m.p.h. and it was driven by a crew of six when used as an "overland train" for the military.

The world's largest railroad station waiting rooms are in Peking Station, Chang'an Boulevard, Peking, China, opened in September 1959, with a capacity of 14,000.

The largest aquarium is the John G. Shedd Aquarium, Chicago. The total capacity of its display tanks is 450,000 gallons.

The most crooked road is Lombard Street in San Francisco between Hyde and Leavenworth. It has 8 consecutive 90-degree turns of 20-ft. radius as it descends steeply one way.

The tallest chimney is the $5½ million International Nickel Company's stack, 1,245 ft. 8 in. tall, at Copper Cliff, Sudbury, Ontario, Canada, completed in 1970. The diameter tapers from 116.4 ft. at the base to 51.8 ft. at the top. It weighs 42,998 tons and became operational in 1971.

THINGS AND PLACES

The largest ancient castle is Prague Castle, Czechoslovakia, originating in the 9th century. It is a very oblong, irregular polygon with an axis of 1,870 ft. and an average traverse diameter of 420 ft., with a surface area of 18 acres.

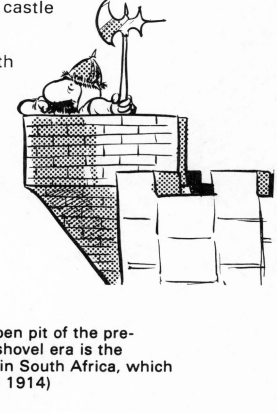

The world's deepest open pit of the pre-mechanical, pick-and-shovel era is the Kimberley Open Mine in South Africa, which took 43 years (1871 to 1914) to dig to a depth of nearly 1,200 feet, with a diameter of about 1,500 feet and a circumference of nearly a mile, covering an area of 36 acres.

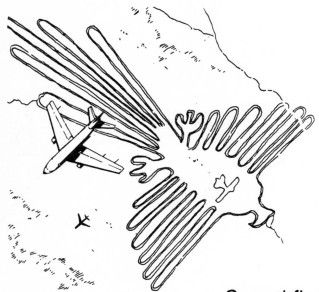

Ground figures in the Nazca
Desert, south of Lima, Peru,
consist of straight lines (one
more than 7 miles long),
geometric shapes and
plants and
animals. Drawn
on the ground by
still unknown per-
sons between 100 B.C.
and 700 A.D. for an
uncertain but probably
religious or astro-
nomical purpose, they
were first detected
from the air *c.* 1928.

THINGS AND PLACES

The largest oil field is
the Ghawar Field,
Saudi Arabia, developed by
ARAMCO, which measures
150 miles by 22 miles.

The earliest
recorded
windmills are
those used for
grinding corn
in Iran
(Persia) in
the 7th
century A.D.

The largest pyramid, and
the largest monument
ever constructed, is the Quetzalcóatl at
Cholula de Rivadabia, 63 miles
southeast of Mexico
City. It is 177 ft.
tall and its
base covers
an area of
nearly 45
acres.

The largest antique ever
sold has been the London
Bridge in March 1968. The sale was made
for $2,460,000. Over 10,000 tons of facade
stonework were reassembled at a cost of
$6,900,000 at Lake Havasu City, Ariz., and
"re-dedicated" Oct. 10, 1971.

THINGS AND PLACES

The country with the greatest recorded number of private dwelling units is India, with 100,251,000 occupied in 1972.

The largest mint in the world is the U.S. Mint in Philadelphia, with an annual capacity on a 3-shift 7-day-a-week production of 8 billion coins. A single stamping machine can produce coins at a rate of 10,000 per hour.

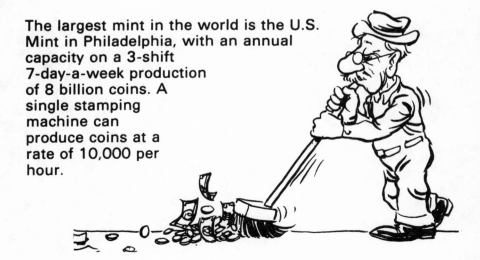

GUINNESS Book of Trivia Records

The auction record for a
toy soldier is $468 for a 3-
inch British Camel Corps lead soldier of
1910, sold at Phillips of London on Aug.
12, 1981.

The yo-yo
originates from a
Filipino jungle fighting
weapon recorded in
the 16th century
weighing 4 lbs.
with a 20-foot
thong. The
word means
"come-come."

The world's lowest firework was George
Plimpton's 40½-inch 720-lb.
Roman candle "Fat Man,"
which was supposed to
break the record over Long
Island, N.Y., in February,
    1975. Instead, it sizzled,
    hissed and exploded,
      leaving a crater 10
      feet deep.

The penknife with the greatest number of blades is the Year Knife made by the cutlers Joseph Rodgers & Sons Ltd., of Sheffield, England. The knife was built in 1822 with 1,822 blades, and was designed to match the year of the Christian era until 2000, but had to halt at 1,973 because there was no more space for blades. Now a way has been found to add blades to 2,000.

The longest pencil, 7 ft. long, was made by the oldest pencil factory, Cumberland in England. It weighed 15¼ lb. and its lead was 1 in. thick.

170

The smallest model aircraft to fly
is one weighing 0.004 oz.
powered by attaching a horsefly
and designed by Don Emmick of
Seattle, Wash. in June, 1979.
One flew for 5 min.

The most expensive writing
pens are the 18-carat
pair of pens (one fiber-
tipped and one ballpoint)
capped by diamonds of
3.88 carats sold
by Alfred
Dunhill Ltd.,
London, for
$22,969 a pair.

The largest sheet of
glass ever
manufactured was one 65 ft. 7 in.
x 8 ft. 2½ in., exhibited by the
Saint Gobain Company in France in
March 1958.

**The largest stained glass window
is complete mural of The
Resurrection Mausoleum,
Justice, Illinois, measuring
22,381 square feet in 2,448
panels completed in 1971.**

TINKLE

TINKLE

The world's largest
chair is the 2,000-
pound, 33-foot-1-
inch-high, 19-foot-7-
inch-wide chair
constructed by
Anniston Steel
& Plumbing Co.,
and completed
in May 1981.

173

The most expensive standard shoes obtainable are the mink-lined golf shoes with 18-karat gold embellishments and ruby-tipped gold spikes by Stylo Matchmakers International Ltd. of Northampton, England, which retail for $9,320 per pair.

The 1887 Jubilee Boot made for the Newark trades procession, Nottinghamshire, England, is 4 feet 3½ inches long and weighs 81¾ lb. It is a size 141, and is owned by Clarks Shoe Museum, Somerset, England.

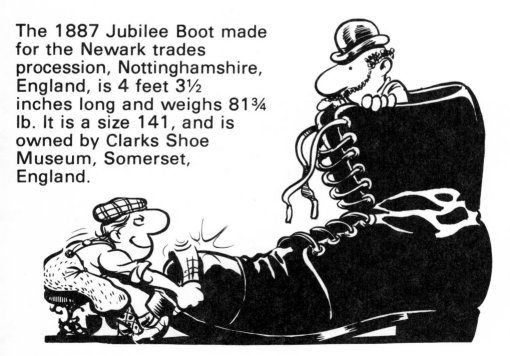

THINGS AND PLACES

The largest blanket ever made
measured 68x100 ft. and weighed
600 lbs. It was knitted in 20,160 6-in.
squares in 10 months (Oct. 1977-
July 1978) by the English *Woman's
Weekly* readers for Action Research
for the
Crippled
Child.

The thickest wire rope ever made is a
spliced crane strop 11¼ inches thick, made
of 2,392 individual wires in March 1979,
by British
Ropes at
Willington
Quay,
Tyneside,
England.

The largest and presumably also the loudest playable guitar is an electric guitar 10 feet 1 inch tall and in excess of 300 pounds in weight built by Sparkling Ragtime Productions of San Francisco and the Guild of American Luthiers, Tacoma, Wash., in December 1980.

The most expensive fabric obtainable is an evening-wear fabric 37½ inches wide, hand embroidered and sequinned on a pure silk ground in a classical flower pattern. It has 194,400 tiny sequins per yard, and is designed by Alan Hershman of London; it cost $550 per meter in May, 1978.

176

The world's largest mineral water firm is
Source Perrier near Nîmes, France with
an annual production of more than 2,100
million bottles, of which
1,200 million now come
from Perrier and Contrexé-
ville. The French
drink 50 liters (106
pints) of mineral
water per person
per year.

6 Humans

The tallest recorded
man of whom there
is irrefutable
evidence was Robert
Wadlow, born in
Alton, Ill., on
February 22, 1918.
He reached a height
of 8 feet 11 inches.

The tallest
(identical) twins
ever recorded were
the Knipe brothers
(b. 1761-*fl.* 1780)
of Magherafelt,
near Londonderry,
Northern Ireland,
who both measured
7 feet 2 inches.

The tallest known living human is Muhammad Alam Channa (b. 1956), who works as an attendant at the shrine of Lal Shahbaz Qalandar in Pakistan. He reached a height of 7 feet by the age of 20. Now age 28, he has reached a height of 8 feet 3 inches.

Anna Hanen Swan (1846-88) of Nova Scotia, Canada, was billed at 8 ft. 1 in. but actually measured 7 ft. 5½ in. In London, June 17, 1871, she married Martin van Buren Bates (1845-1919), of Whitesburg, Letcher County, Ky., who stood 7 ft. 2½ in., making them the tallest married couple on record.

The tallest soldier of all time was Väinö Myllyrinne (1909-63) who was inducted into the Finnish Army when he was 7 ft. 3 in. and later grew to 8 ft. 1¼ in.

The greatest estimated weight attributed to any human by a member of the medical profession is 1,400 lbs. for John Brower Minnoch (b. 1941) whose height was measured to be 6 feet 1 inch lying down. He was carried into University Hospital, Seattle, Washington, on planking in March, 1978. His weight by July, 1979, was down to a measured 475 lbs.

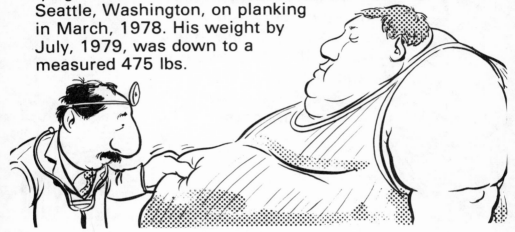

The claimed waist measurement of Robert Earl Hughes (b. 1926) was 122 inches, the greatest on record. Hughes, the heaviest medically weighed human, weighed 1,041 pounds at the time of his death in 1958.

The heaviest twins are the performers Billy and Benny McCrary, *alias* Billy and Benny McGuire (born 1948) of Hendersonville, North Carolina, whose weights fluctuate between 720 and 740 lbs. Since they have difficulty walking they ride their mini-bikes everywhere, even indoors.

In Chungchon, South Korea, it was reported in September 1981 that there was unaccountably 38 pairs of twins in only 275 families — the highest ratio ever recorded.

The greatest recorded weight differential
for a married couple is 922 lb. in the
case of Mills Darden (1,020 lb.) of
North Carolina and his wife Mary
(98 lb.). Despite her diminutiveness,
however, Mrs. Darden bore her
husband at least three (and
possibly five) children
before her death in 1837.

The smallest recorded waist among women of normal stature in the 20th century is a reputed 13 inches in the cases of the French actress Mlle Polaire (1881-1939) and Mrs. Ethel Granger (1905-82) of Peterborough, England, who reduced from a natural 22 inches over the period 1929-39.

The speed record for slimming was established by Paul M. Kimelman, 21, of Pittsburgh, Pa., who from Dec. 25, 1966, to Aug. 1967, went on a crash diet of 300 to 600 calories per day to reduce from 487 lb. to 130 lb., a total loss of 357 lb.

The maximum measured extension of the neck by the successive fitting of copper coils, as practiced by the Padaung or Karen people of Burma, is 15¾ inches. The neck muscles become so atrophied that the removal of the support of the rings produces asphyxiation.

An experiment on Yorkshire TV in England on August 17, 1978, showed that when Sue Evans, 17, was fired from a cannon, she was 3/8 inch shorter in height on landing.

The smallest pygmies are the Mbuti, with an average height of 4 feet 6 inches for men and 4 feet 5 inches for women. They live in the forests near the river Ituri in the Congo (Kinshasa), Africa.

The thinnest recorded adults of normal height are those suffering from Simmonds' disease (Hypophyseal cachexia). Edward C. Hagner (1892-1962), *alias* Eddie Masher, is alleged to have weighed only 48 lbs. at a height of 5 feet 7 inches. He was also known as "the Skeleton Dude."

Dreaming sleep is characterized by rapid eye movements (called REM). The longest recorded period of REM is 2 hours 23 minutes, set by Bill Carskadon on February 15, 1967, at the Deparment of Psychology, University of Illinois, Chicago. His previous sleep had been interrupted.

Research at the Ear, Nose and Throat Department of St. Mary's Hospital, London, shows that a rasping snore can attain a loudness of 69 decibels, as compared to 70 to 90 decibels for a pneumatic drill.

The longest moustache on record was that of Masuriya Din (b. 1908), a Brahmin of the Partabgarh district in Uttar Pradesh, India. It grew to an extended span of 102 in. between 1949 and 1962.

The longest known set of nails now belongs to the left hand of Shridhar Chillal, of Poona, India. The five nails on his left hand, by March 21, 1982, had achieved a measured aggregate length of 116½ inches.

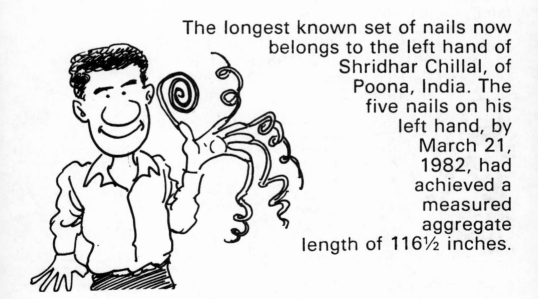

The earliest recorded self-made millionairess was Madame Charles Joseph Walker *(nee* Sarah Breedlove on December 23, 1867), whose fortune was founded on a hair straightener. She had been a scrubwoman and a laundress.

The only verified example of a family producing five single children with coincidental birthdays is that of Catherine (1952), Carol (1953), Charles (1956), Claudia (1961) and Cecilia (1966), born to Ralph and Carolyn Cummins of Clintwood, Va., all on Feb. 20th.

The longest recorded
attack of hiccoughs is
that afflicting Charles
Osborne (b. 1894) of
Anthon, Iowa, from
1922 to date. He
contracted it when
slaughtering a hog.
His first wife left
him and he is
unable to keep in his
false teeth.

Jack V. and Edna Moran of Seattle, Wash., have married each other 40 times since the original occasion on July 27, 1937, in Seaside, Ore. Subsequent ceremonies have included those at Banff, Canada (1952), Cairo, Egypt (1966) and Westminster Abbey, London (1975).

The shortest valid will in the world is "Vse zene," the Czech for "All to wife," written and dated January 19, 1967, by Herr Karl Tausch of Langen, Hesse, Germany.

196

The longest
engagement on record
is one of 67 years
between Octavio
Guillen, 82, and
Adriana Martinez,
82. They finally
took the plunge
in June
1969, in
Mexico City.

Mrs. Beverly Nina Avery, then aged 48, a barmaid
from Los Angeles, set a monogamous world
record in October, 1957, by obtaining her 16th
divorce, this one from her 14th husband. She
alleged outside the court that five of the 14 had
broken her nose.

Two brothers, Sven and Per, and a sister, Kari, Heistad of Lebanon, N.H., have never slept indoors since March 1974. The coldest they have experienced has been Christmas morning 1980 with a wind chill temperature of –67°F, which to them is a "three-bag night."

The world's leading bird-watcher is G. Stuart Keith, an Englishman who works at the America Museum of Natural History, New York City. In the 32 years to March, 1979, his score is 5,450 species of the 8,650 known species.

The most protracted yodel on record was that of Errol Bird for 10 hours 15 mins. in Lisburn, N. Ireland, Oct. 6, 1979.

The normal intelligible outdoor range of the male human voice in still air is 200 yards. The *silbo,* the whistled language of the Spanish-speaking Canary Island of La Gomera, is intelligible across the valleys, under ideal conditions, at 5 miles.

The claim for the
greatest recorded fall
survived by a mountaineer
is for Christopher Timms
(Canterbury University)
who is supposed to have
slid 7,500 feet down an ice face
into a crevasse on Mt. Elie de
Beaumont (10,200 feet), New
Zealand on December 7, 1966.
He survived with concussions, bruises
and a hand injury.

The highest recorded total of pills, swallowed by a patient is 331,211 from June 9, 1967 to January 1, 1979, by C. H. A. Kilner of Malawi, following a successful pancreatectomy.

The greatest depth of an actual escape without any equipment has been from 225 feet by Richard A. Slater from the rammed submersible *Nekton Beta* off Catalina Island, Calif., on Sept. 28, 1970.

Brother Giovanni Battista Orsenigo, Rome, Italy, a religious dentist, conserved all the teeth he extracted during the time he exercised his profession from 1868 to 1904. In 1903, the number was counted and found to be 2,000,744 teeth.

The record for persistence in taking and failing a test for a driver's license is held by Mrs. Miriam Hargrave (b. Apr. 3, 1908) of Wakefield, Yorkshire, England, who failed her 39th driving test in 8 years on Apr. 29, 1970, when she "crashed" through a set of red lights. She finally passed her 40th driving test on Aug. 3, 1970.

Henrietta (Hetty) Howland
Green (1835-1916), who
kept a balance of over
$31,400,000 in one bank
alone, was so stingy that
her son had to have his
leg amputated
because of the
delays in
finding a *free*
medical
clinic.

An early Rubik's cube
speed contest (with
standard dislocation and inspection
time) held in Munich, West Germany,
March 13, 1981, resulted in a 38.0-
second tie between Ronald Brinkman
and Jury Fröschl.

The longest recorded handwritten letter-writing marathon was one of 505 hours and more than 3,998 letters and their envelopes by Raymond L. Cantwell of Oxford, England, Aug. 25-Sept. 16, 1978.

The most protracted pinball marathon was one of 216 hours played by Jon Wood and David Irvine (each playing separately) of Luton, Bedfordshire, England, March 1-9, 1979.

The title of world champion hitchhiker is claimed by Devon Smith, who from 1947 to 1971 thumbed lifts totaling 291,000 miles.

The longest taxi journey on record was begun in Hoboken, New Jersey, on September 9, 1976, when Mrs. Ann Drache and Mrs. Nesta Sgro hired Jack Keator to drive them 6,752 miles through 15 states for an agreed fare of $2,500. They arrived back in Hoboken on October 6, 1976.

The greatest exponent of reverse pedestrianism has been Plennie L. Wingo, then of Abilene, Texas, who started on his 8,000-mile transcontinental walk on April 15, 1931, from Santa Monica, California, to Istanbul, Turkey, and arrived on October 24, 1932. He celebrated the walk's 45th anniversary by covering the 452 miles from Santa Monica to San Francisco, California, backwards, in 85 days, aged 81 years.

GUINNESS Book of Trivia Records

An unnamed Italian
industrialist was
reported to have lost $1,920,000 in
five hours at roulette in Monte
Carlo, Monaco, on March 6, 1974.

The greatest amount paid by a single
check in the history of banking was one
equivalent to $2,046,700,000, handed
over by Daniel P. Moynihan, the U.S.
ambassador to India, in New Delhi on
February 18, 1974.

Eugene Schneider of Carteret, New Jersey,
allegedly cut his $80,000 home in half with
a chain saw in July, 1976,
after his wife sued him for
divorce, thus fulfilling in
his eyes the equal
division of property
required by New
Jersey law.

GUINNESS Book of Trivia Records

The pay phone with the heaviest
usage is one in the Greyhound bus
terminal in Chicago, which
averages 270 calls a day, and is
thus used each 5 min. 20 sec.
around the clock all year.

It is recorded that
Johann Heinrich Karl
Thieme, sexton of Aldenburg,
Germany, dug 23,311 graves during
a 50-year career. In 1826, his
understudy dug *his* grave.

On August 12, 1975, William De Palma of California, agreed to a $750,000 settlement for 16 months' wrongful imprisonment in McNeil Island Federal Prison, Washington. He had been given a 15-year sentence for armed robbery on forged fingerprint evidence in 1968.

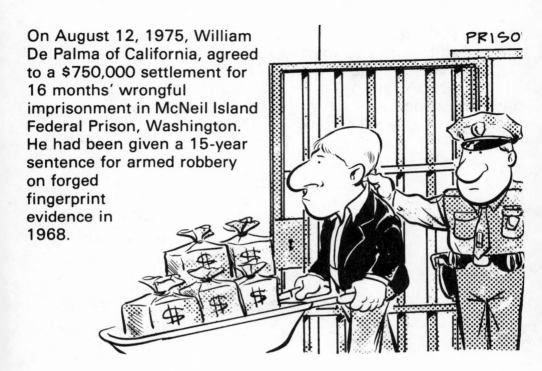

The most prolific suggestion box stuffer on record is John Drayton (b. Sept. 18, 1907) of Newport, Gwent, Wales, who has plied British Rail and the companies from which it was formed with a total of 28,777 suggestions from 1924 to May 1980. One out of every seven was accepted.

211

A judge of the Court of Session of Scotland has sent the editors his candidate for the most inexplicable law, which reads, "In the Nuts (unground), (other than ground nuts) Order, the expression nuts shall have reference to such nuts, other than ground nuts, as would but for this amending Order not qualify as nuts (unground) (other than ground nuts) by reason of their being nuts (unground)."

The first recorded one-man audience occurred at the Oldham Grange Arts Centre, Lancashire, England, on Oct. 23, 1980, when Ronald Bradbury made theatrical history by sitting through "Oh Mistress Mine" as the sole spectator, while the show went on.

Laos is the only country presently without coins (paper money only). Kampuchea (Cambodia) abolished money under the Pol Pot regime in 1975, but reintroduced it in March 1980 with the riel as the monetary unit.

The holed stone discs used for money on the island of Yap are the most massive coins ever known. The stone discs vary in size from "small change" of less than 9 inches in diameter to cartwheel-size stones 12 feet across.

The most extreme recorded case of academic juvenility was that of William Thomson (1824-1907), later Lord Kelvin, who entered Glasgow University aged 10 years 4 months in Oct. 1834, and matriculated on Nov. 14, 1834.

The most northerly university is Inupiat University of the Arctic at Barrow, Alaska on Lat. 71°16'N. Eskimo subjects are featured in the curriculum.

There are believed to be 20 or more languages, including 6 North American Indian languages, in which no one can converse, because there is only one speaker left alive. Eyak is still spoken in southeast Alaska by two aged sisters if they meet.

The greatest land auction ever was that at Anchorage, Alaska, in 1969, for 450,858 acres of the oil-bearing North Slope. A price of $28,233 per acre for a 2,560-acre lease was bid by the Amerada Hess Corp.-Getty Oil consortium.

GUINNESS Book of Trivia Records

The largest pleasure beach is Virginia Beach, Va. It has 28 miles of beach front on the Atlantic and 10 miles of estuary frontage. The area embraces 255 sq. mi. and contains 134 hotels and motels.

Reclamation Plant No. 1, Fresh Kills, Staten Island, N.Y., opened in March 1974, is the world's largest sanitary landfill. In its first 4 months, 500,000 tons of refuse was dumped on the site.

The most densely populated territory in the world is the Portuguese province of Macau (or Macao), on the southern coast of China. It has an estimated population of 289,000 (mid-1977) in an area of 6.2 square miles, giving a density of 46,600 per square mile.

The country with the most dentists is the United States, where 138,000 were registered members of the American Dental Association in 1980.

The highest inhabited buildings are those in the Indian-Tibet border fort of Bāsisi at *c.* 19,700 ft.

The longest place name now in use is Taumatawhakatangihangakoauauotamatea (turipukakapikimaungahoronuku) pokaiwhenuakitanatahu, the unofficial 85-letter version of the name of a hill in the Southern Hawke's Bay district of North Island, New Zealand. This Maori name means "the hill whereon was played the flute of Tamatea, circumnavigator of lands, for his lady love."

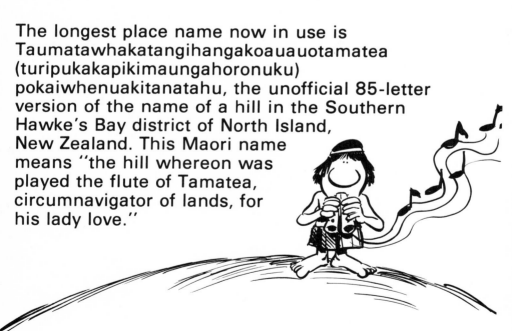

Statisticians contend that Bolivia,
since it became a sovereign country
in 1825, has had 189 *coups d'état.*

The practice of
numbering
houses began in
1463 on the Pont
Notre Dame,
Paris, France.

The highest *shade* temperature ever recorded was 136.4°F at Al' Aziziyah, Libya, on Sept. 13, 1922.

The longest fashion show ever recorded was one which lasted for 48 hours on The Roseland catwalk, Sydney, Australia, on June 16-18, 1977. Three models and the MC walked 41.4 miles.

The most evil-smelling substance, of the 17,000 smells so far classified, must be a matter of opinion, but ethyl mercaptan and butyl seleno-mercaptan are powerful claimants, each with a smell reminiscent of a combination of rotting cabbage, garlic, onions and sewer gas.

GUINNESS Book of Trivia Records

A prime number is any positive integer (excluding 1) having no integral factors other than itself and unity, *e.g.* 2, 3, 5, 7, or 11. The lowest prime number is 2. The highest known prime number is a number of 13,395 digits, discovered on Apr. 8, 1979, after a 2-month-long run on a Cray One Computer at the University of California by Harry Nelson, 47, and David Slowinski, 25.

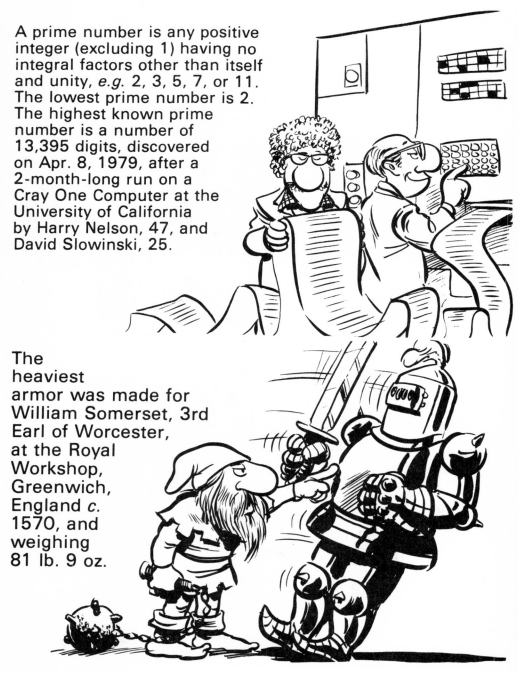

The heaviest armor was made for William Somerset, 3rd Earl of Worcester, at the Royal Workshop, Greenwich, England *c.* 1570, and weighing 81 lb. 9 oz.

The longest
recorded reign
of any
monarch is
that of Pepi II,
a Sixth Dynasty
Pharaoh of
ancient Egypt.
His reign began
in *c.* 2310 B.C.
when he was 6,
and lasted *c.*
94 years.

The longest speech
made in the United
Nations was one of 4 hours
29 minutes by the
president of Cuba,
Fidel Castro Ruz
in August 1960.

Of the world's 26 monarchies, the one with the youngest king is Bhutan (in the Himalayas) where King Jigme Singye Wangchuk (born November 11, 1955) succeeded to the throne on July 24, 1972.

Emperor Trajan of Rome (98-117 A.D.) staged a display involving 4,941 pairs of gladiators over 117 days. Publius Ostorius, a freedman, survived 51 combats in Pompeii.

The most successful dog trainer — and the fastest — is Mrs. Barbara Woodhouse of Rickmansworth, Hertfordshire, England, who has trained 17,136 dogs to obey the basic commands during the period from 1951 to Mar. 25, 1982. Her record for a single day is 80 dogs in June 1973 in Denver, Colo.

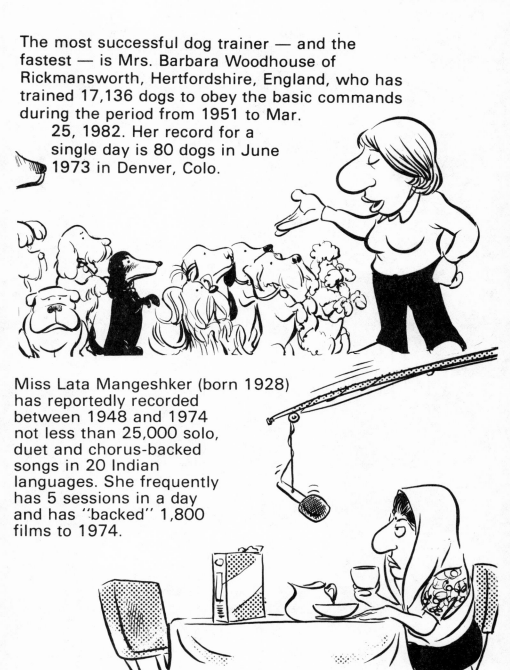

Miss Lata Mangeshker (born 1928) has reportedly recorded between 1948 and 1974 not less than 25,000 solo, duet and chorus-backed songs in 20 Indian languages. She frequently has 5 sessions in a day and has "backed" 1,800 films to 1974.

7   Sports and Games

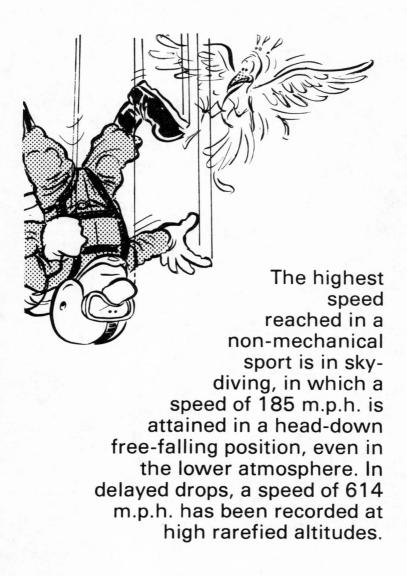

The highest speed reached in a non-mechanical sport is in sky-diving, in which a speed of 185 m.p.h. is attained in a head-down free-falling position, even in the lower atmosphere. In delayed drops, a speed of 614 m.p.h. has been recorded at high rarefied altitudes.

The oldest person to break a world record is Irish-born John J. Flanagan (1868-1938), triple Olympic hammer throw champion for the U.S., 1900-1908, who set his last world record of 184 feet 4 inches at New Haven, Connecticut, on July 24, 1909, aged 41 years 196 days.

The steepest mountain slope, Mount Rakaposhi (25,498 ft.), rises 19,652 ft. from the Hunza Valley, Pakistan, with an overall gradient of 31° over a distance of 32,808 ft.

The greatest fortune amassed by an individual in sport is an estimated $47,500,000 by Sonja Henie (1912-69), of Norway, the triple Olympic figure skating champion (1928-32-36) as a professional ice skating promoter starring in her own ice shows and 11 films.

The greatest number of world titles in archery ever won by a man is four by H. Deutgen (Sweden) in 1947–48–49–50.

Sultan Selim III shot an arrow 1,400 Turkish *pikes* or *gez* near Istanbul, Turkey, in 1798. The equivalent English distance is somewhere between 953 and 972 yards.

Charlotte "Lottie" Dod (1871-1960) won the Wimbledon singles title (1887 to 1893) 5 times, the British Ladies Golf Championship in 1904, an Olympic silver medal for archery in 1908, and represented England at hockey in 1899. She also excelled at skating and tobogganing.

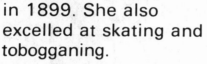

The longest flight shooting records are achieved in the footbow class. In the unlimited footbow division, the professional Harry Drake of Lakeside, California, holds the record at 1 mile 268 yards, shot at Ivanpah Dry Lake, California, on October 24, 1971.

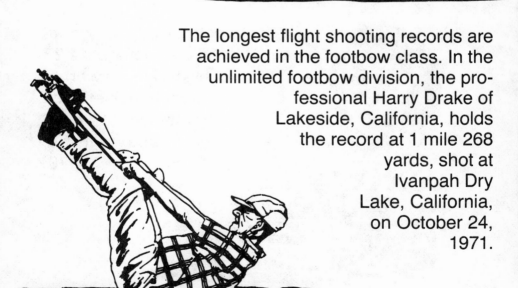

The Indianapolis 500-mile race (200 laps) was inaugurated on May 30, 1911. The most successful driver has been Anthony Joseph "A.J." Foyt, Jr., who won in 1961, 1964, 1967 and 1977.

The greatest number of Grand Prix victories is 27 by Jackie Stewart of Scotland between September 12, 1965 and August 5, 1973.

Baseball Origins: The Rev. Thomas Wilson, of Maidstone, Kent, England, wrote disapprovingly, in 1700, of baseball being played on Sundays. It is also referred to in *Northanger Abbey* by Jane Austen, *c.* 1798.

Ron Hunt, an infielder who played with various National League teams from 1963 to 1974, led the league in getting hit by pitched balls for a record seven consecutive years. His career total is 243, also a major league record.

The littlest major leaguer was Eddie Gaedel, a 3-ft., 7-in., 65-lb. midget. In 1951 he walked on four pitches in his only major league appearance.

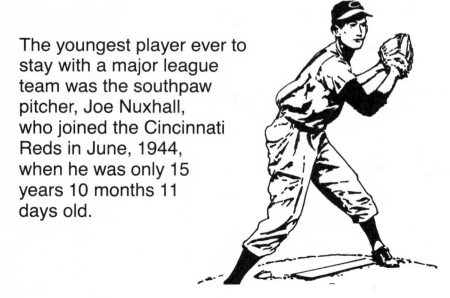

The youngest player ever to stay with a major league team was the southpaw pitcher, Joe Nuxhall, who joined the Cincinnati Reds in June, 1944, when he was only 15 years 10 months 11 days old.

Joe Sprinz of the San Francisco Seals, Pacific Coast League, caught a baseball (on his fifth attempt) dropped 1,000 feet from an airship to set a record for a catch from the greatest height. He accomplished this lofty task on August 3, 1939, at Treasure Island in San Francisco Bay. The force of catching the ball cost him 4 front teeth.

The greatest batter in baseball history was Ty Cobb, who holds the records for highest lifetime batting average (.367), most base hits (4,191) and most runs scored (2,244).

Mickey Mantle, slugging champ of the New York Yankees, holds the World Series records, in games played between 1951 and 1964, for most runs (42), most RBI's (40) and most home runs (18). He was also one of six players voted MVP three times — in 1956, '57 and '62.

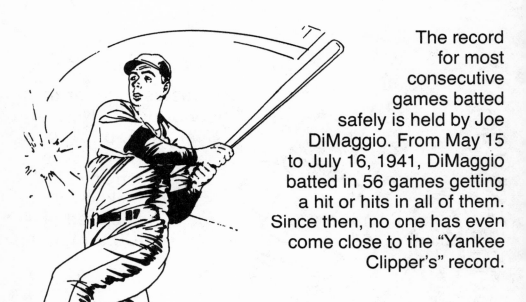

The record for most consecutive games batted safely is held by Joe DiMaggio. From May 15 to July 16, 1941, DiMaggio batted in 56 games getting a hit or hits in all of them. Since then, no one has even come close to the "Yankee Clipper's" record.

It's going . . . going . . . gone! Henry L. (Hank) Aaron has heard that phrase more times than any player. Aaron broke the record set by George H. (Babe) Ruth of 714 home runs in a lifetime when he hit No. 715, April 8, 1974.

His total at the end of the 1975 season was 733 four-baggers.

237

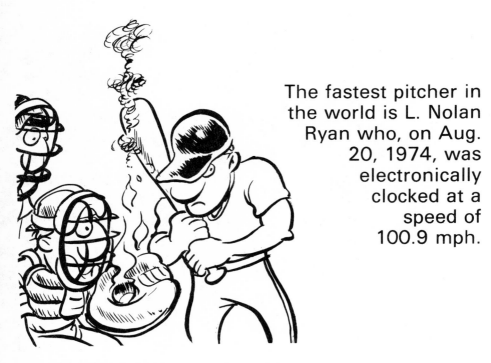

The fastest pitcher in the world is L. Nolan Ryan who, on Aug. 20, 1974, was electronically clocked at a speed of 100.9 mph.

The longest throw of a 5-5¼-oz. baseball is 445 ft. 10 in. by Glen Gorbous Aug. 1, 1957. Mildred "Babe" Didrikson (1914-56) threw a ball 296 feet at Jersey City, N.J., July 25, 1931.

Hoyt Wilhelm pitched the most games of any pitcher in the major leagues. In 21 seasons with ten different teams in both leagues, he pitched in 1,070 games.

Don Larsen of the N.Y. Yankees did not allow a single Brooklyn Dodger to reach first base when he pitched the only perfect game ever seen in a World Series on October 8, 1956.

239

Josh Gibson hit 800 lifetime home runs for the Homestead Grays of the Negro League, and 84 in one season. He was never able to play in the major leagues, but was posthumously elected to the Baseball Hall of Fame in 1972.

The most expensive basketball player is Moses Malone who was 19 when he left the University of Maryland and signed a 7-year contract to play basketball with the Utah Stars of the A.B.A. in August, 1974. He received a reported three million dollar contract.

The highest score by an individual player in a basketball game occurred in a college game when Clarence (Bevo) Francis of Rio Grande College, Rio Grande, Ohio, scored 150 points in a game in 1954.

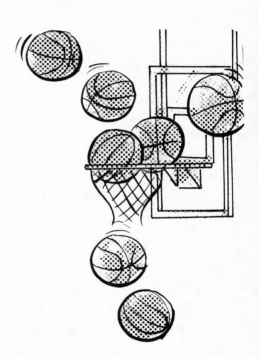

The tallest basketball player of all time is reputed to be Suleiman Ali Nashnush (b. 1943) who played for the Libyan team in 1962 when he measured 8 ft. tall.

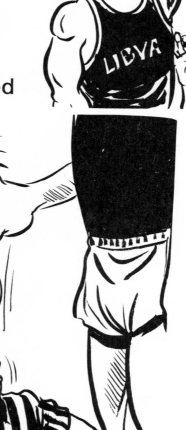

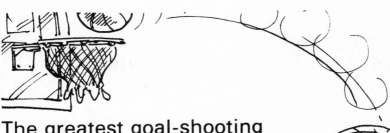

The greatest goal-shooting basketball demonstration was made by a professional, Ted St. Martin, now of Jacksonville, Fla., who, on June 25, 1977, scored 2,036 consecutive free throws. St. Martin made 258 free throws (of 297 attempts) in 10 minutes in Orange Park, Fla., on Nov. 13, 1982.

The record for consecutive strikes in sanctioned match bowling is 33 by John Pezzin (b. 1930) at Toledo, Ohio, on March 4, 1976.

The first world heavyweight title fight, with gloves and 3-minute rounds, was between John L. Sullivan and "Gentleman" James J. Corbett in New Orleans, on Sept. 7, 1892. Corbett won in 21 rounds.

The longest recorded fight with gloves was between Andy Bowen of New Orleans and Jack Burke in New Orleans, Apr. 6-7, 1893. The fight lasted 110 rounds (7 hours 19 min. from 9:15 p.m. to 4:34 a.m.) but was declared no contest (later changed to a draw) when both men were unable to continue.

The smallest man to win any world boxing has been Pascual Perez (b. Mendoza, Argentina) who won the flyweight title in Tokyo on November 26, 1954, at 107 lbs. and 4 feet 11½ inches.

Only Rocky Marciano shares with Gene Tunney the honor of *finally* retiring as an undefeated heavyweight champion.

The youngest age at which a world boxing title has been won is 21 years 331 days by Floyd Patterson (b. Waco, N.C., Jan. 4, 1935), who won the vacant title by beating Archie Moore in 5 rounds in Chicago on Nov. 30, 1956.

SPORTS AND GAMES

The acknowledged pioneer of
canoeing as a modern sport was
John Macgregor, a British barrister,
in 1865. The Canoe Club was
formed on July
26, 1866.

Beatrice and John Dowd, Ken Beard and Steve
Benson (Richard Gillett replaced him mid-journey)
paddled 1,559 miles out of a total journey of 2,010
miles from Venezuela to Miami, Fla., via the West
Indies from Aug. 11, 1977, to April 29, 1978, in
two Klepper Aerius
20 kayaks.

Two fencers began their careers at age 17. One, Ramón Fonst of Cuba, in 1900 won his first Olympic gold medal. Edoardo Mangiarotti of Italy was 17 when he won two Olympic competitions in the foil and épée in 1936.

The longest fresh-water cast ratified under International Casting Federation rules is 574 feet 2 inches by Walter Kummerow (West Germany), for the Bait Distance Double-Handed 30-gram event held at Lenzerheide, Switzerland, in the 1968 Championship.

The longest recorded fight
between a fisherman and a
fish is 32 hours 5 minutes
by Donal Heatley
with a black marlin
(estimated length
20 feet and weight
1,500 lbs.) off
Mayor Island off
Tauranga, New
Zealand, Jan. 21-22,
1968. It towed the
12-ton launch 50
miles before breaking
the line.

ABU-Garcia, a leading manufacturer of fishing tackle, offered a $250,000 reward for landing an all-tackle world record fish in one of four categories. Al McReynolds, 36, in Atlantic City, N.J., on the night of Sept. 21, 1982, hooked and, after a 2-hour fight, landed a 78-lb., 8-oz. striped bass—a world record for rod and reel. On Feb. 11, 1983, McReynolds received a check for $250,000 —the most money ever paid for a fish.

SPORTS AND GAMES

The longest punt was one of 98 yards, by Steve O'Neal of the N.Y. Jets in a game against Denver on Sept. 21, 1969 (AFL).

The most fumbles in one professional football season were made by Dan Pastorini, of Houston, in 1973. He fumbled 17 times.

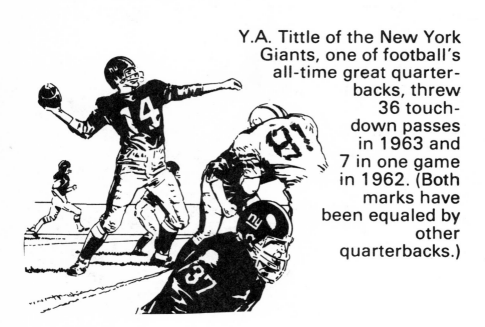

Sammy Baugh (Wash.) was the most efficient football passer, with a 70.3 percentage for the season in 1945. He also led the league in passing for six seasons between 1937 and 1949.

Y.A. Tittle of the New York Giants, one of football's all-time great quarterbacks, threw 36 touchdown passes in 1963 and 7 in one game in 1962. (Both marks have been equaled by other quarterbacks.)

The
longest straight
hole shot in one is the 10th
hole (447 yds.) at Miracle
Hills Golf Club, Omaha, Neb.
Robert Mitera achieved a
hole-in-one there on Oct. 7,
1965. Mitera, aged 21 and 5
ft. 6 in. tall, weighed 165
lbs. A two-handicap player,
he normally drove 245 yd.
A 50-mph gust carried his
shot over a 290-yd. drop-off.

The world record for a golf drive is 392 yds., by a member of the Irish PGA, Tommie Campbell (Foxrock Golf Club), made at Dun Laoghaire, Dublin, in July 1964.

Professional golfer Art Wall, Jr. holds a record for having hit 41 holes-in-one in his career.

SPORTS AND GAMES

The lowest recorded score for throwing a golf ball around 18 holes (over 6,000 yards) is 82 by Joe Flynn, 21, at the 6,228-yard Port Royal Course, Bermuda, on March 27, 1975.

The record for 2-arm chins from a dead hang position is 135 by Joe Hernandez at Dysart Junior H.S., Cashion, Ariz., on May 22, 1980. William Aaron Vaught did 20 one-arm chin-ups at Finch's Gymnasium, Houston, Tex., on Jan. 3, 1976.

The best standing high jump is 6 ft. 2¾ in. by Rune Almen at Karlstad, Sweden, on May 30, 1980.

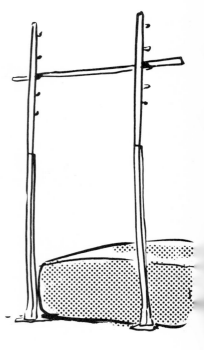

Fred Kueffer did 265 consecutive handstand push-ups at Kellogg H.S., Little Canada, Minn. where he is gymnastic coach, on Nov. 10, 1981.

Don Perry of Champaign, Ill., climbed 20 ft. of rope (using only his hands) in 2.8 seconds.

The longest recorded non-stop rope-jumping marathon was one of 9 hours 46 mins. by Katsumi Suzuki, in Kumagaya Gymnasium, Saitama, Japan, on March 23, 1980.

Ashrita Furman performed
6,773 forward rolls over 10
miles in Central Park, N.Y.C.,
on Nov. 19, 1980.

Colin Hewick, 23, set the record
when he did 10,029 consecutive
gymnastic push-ups at the South
Holderness Sports Centre,
Humberside,
England, on
July 18,
1982.

Gymnast Larissa
Latynina of the U.S.S.R. has
won six individual and three
team gold medals, five silver,
and four bronze for an
all-time record total of 18
Olympic medals.

Nadia Comaneci (b. 1962,
Rumania) became the first
gymnast to be awarded a
perfect score of 10.00 in
the Olympic Games, in the
1976 Montreal Olympics.
She ended the
competition with a
total of seven
such marks.

Terry Lemus performs a difficult triple back somersault with 1½ twists in her trapeze act at Circus Circus Hotel in Las Vegas, Nevada.

The highest speed measured for any ice hockey player is 29.7 m.p.h. for Bobby Hull (Chicago Black Hawks) (b. January 3, 1939). The highest puck speed is also attributed to Hull, whose left-handed slap shot has been measured at 118.3 m.p.h.

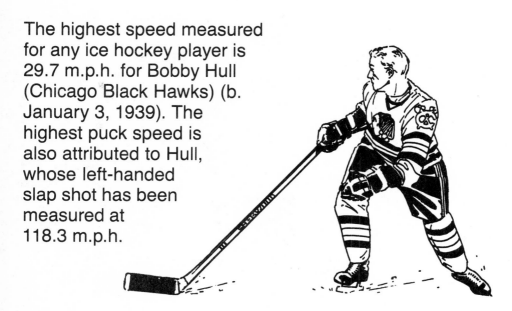

There is pictorial evidence of
hockey being played on ice in the
Netherlands in the 17th century.
The game probably was first
played in 1860 in Kingston, Ontario, Canada, but Montreal and
Halifax also lay claim to priority.

The youngest jockey ever to race was Frank Wooton who rode his first winner in South Africa when he was 9 years 10 months. He later went on to become an English champion jockey, 1909-12.

The lightest recorded jockey was Kitchener (died 1872), who won the Chester Cup in England on *Red Deer* in 1844 at 49 lbs.

The sport of pitching horseshoes was derived by military farriers and is of great antiquity. The first formal World Championships were staged at Bronson, Kansas, in 1909.

The longest continuous session of horseshoe pitching is 100 hours by a team of 6 playing in shifts in Allentown, Pennsylvania, August 6-10, 1973.

265

The largest artificial outdoor ice rink
is the quintuple complex of the
Fujikyu Highland Promenade Rink,
Japan (opened 1967),
with an area
of 285,244
square feet.

The most Olympic gold
medals won in speed
skating is six by
Lydia Skoblikova
(born March 8,
1939), of Chel-
yaminsk,
U.S.S.R., in
1960 (two) and
1964 (four).

The fastest throw of a
(pelota) ball was made by
Jose Ramon Areitio at
an electronically
measured speed of
180 m.p.h., recorded
at the Palm Beach
Jai-Alai, Florida,
on June 1,
1977.

The largest field for any ball game is that for polo with 12.4 acres.

The longest recorded lacrosse throw is 162.86 yards, by Barney Quinn of Ottawa, Canada, on September 10, 1892.

Jacqueline Smith (G.B.) (b. March 29, 1951) scored 10 consecutive dead center strikes (4-in. disk) in the World Championships at Zagreb, Yugoslavia, Sept. 1, 1978.

Michael Eufemia holds the record for the greatest continuous run in a straight pool match, pocketing 625 balls without a miss on Feb. 2, 1960 before a large crowd at Logan's Billiard Academy, Brooklyn, N.Y.

The world's record for rope quoit throwing is an unbroken sequence of 4,002 pegs by Bill Irby, Sr., of Australia in 1968.

270

The top bucking bull was probably *Honky Tonk,* an 11-year-old Brahma, who unseated 187 riders in an undefeated eight-year career to his retirement in September 1978.

The youngest winner of a world rodeo title is Metha Brorsen of Oklahoma, who was only 11 years old when she won the International Rodeo Association Cowgirls barrel racing event in 1975.

GUINNESS Book of Trivia Records

The largest indoor roller skating rink ever to operate was located in the Grand Hall, Olympia, London. It had an actual skating area of 68,000 square feet. It first opened in 1890 for one season; then again from 1909 to 1912.

Theodore J. Coombs of Hermosa Beach, Calif., skated 5,193 miles from Los Angeles to New York City and back to Yates Center, Kan., from May 30 to Sept. 14, 1979.

The youngest Olympic Gold Medalist ever was a French boy (whose name is not recorded) who coxed the Netherlands coxed pair in 1900. He was not more than 10 and may have been as young as 7. He substituted for Dr. Hermanus Brockmann, who coxed in the heats but proved too heavy.

Rowing alone in a singles scull, Jack Bereford, Jnr., of Great Britain, won the major sculls race 7 times and took Olympic gold medals three times between 1920 and 1936.

273

The longest annual rowing race is the Ringvaart Regatta, a 62-mile contest for eights held at Delft, Netherlands. The record time is 7 hours 3 minutes 29 seconds by the Njord team on May 31, 1979.

The *Round the Bays* 6.5-mile run in Auckland, N.Z. attracted an estimated 70,000 runners on March 28, 1981. The most runners in a marathon were the 16,350 in the London Marathon on May 9, 1982, of whom 15,758 finished.

The annual Housewives Pancake Race at Olney, Buckinghamshire, England, was first mentioned in 1445. The record for the winding 415-yard course (three tosses mandatory) is 61.0 seconds, set by Sally Ann Faulkner, 16, on February 26, 1974. The record for the counterpart race at Liberal, Kansas, is 59.1 seconds by Kathleen West, 19, on February 10, 1970.

The largest recorded field in any cross-country race was 10,055 starters in the 18.6-mile Lidingöloppet, near Stockholm, Sweden, on Oct. 4, 1981. There were 9,650 finishers.

Duncan McLean of Scotland set a world age — 92 — record of 100 meters in 21.7 seconds in August 1977.

SPORTS AND GAMES

In the ancient Olympic Games, Leonidas of Rhodos won 12 running titles from 164 to 152 B.C.

The continuous duration record (i.e. no rest breaks) for scuba without surface air hoses is 72 hours 2 minutes by Valene E. Willhite of Athol, Mass., Sept. 16-19, 1982.

Skateboarding. Trevor Baxter high jumped 5 ft. 4 in. at Farnborough, England, on July 26, 1981.

Yuichiro Miura (Japan) skied 1.6 miles down Mt. Everest on May 6, 1970, starting from 26,574 ft., highest recorded starting point for a skier.

SPORTS AND GAMES

The longest chair lift in the world is the Alpine Way to Kosciusko Châlet lift above Thredbo, near the Snowy Mountains, N.S.W., Australia. It takes from 45 to 75 mins. to ascend the 3.5 miles, according to the weather.

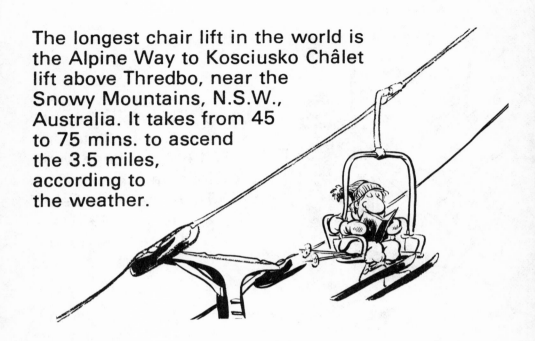

Sylvan Saudan (Switzerland) achieved a descent of Mont Blanc from 13,937 feet on October 17, 1967, skiing gradients in excess of 60 degrees.

The World Cup of skiing, instituted in 1967, has been won four times by Gustav Thoni (Italy), (b. February 28, 1931) in 1971–72–73–75.

The most Olympic gold medals won by an individual for skiing is four (including one for a relay) by Sixten Jernberg (born February 6, 1929), of Sweden, in 1956-60-64. In addition, Jernberg has won three silver and two bronze medals.

SPORTS AND GAMES

The greatest recorded vertical descent in
parachute ski-jumping is 3,300 ft. by Rick
Sylvester, who on July 28, 1976, skied off the
6,600 ft. summit of Mt. Asgard in Auyuittuq
National Park, Baffin Island, Canada. The
jump was made for a
sequence in the
James Bond
film *The
Spy
Who
Loved
Me.*

The fastest officially recorded time for covering a mile on snowshoes is 6 min. 23.8 sec. by Richard Lemay at Manchester, N.H., in 1973.

The soccer player credited with the most career goals is Pelé, who, for the greater part of his 20-year career has averaged a goal a match. His total before he came to play in the U.S. in 1975 was 1,216.

282

The fastest goal in World
Cup soccer competition
was one in 30 seconds by Olle Nyberg
for Sweden vs.
Hungary, in Paris,
June 16, 1938.

A soccer match between the Simon
Fraser University Clansmen and
the Quincy College Hawks
lasted 4 hours 25 minutes
(221 minutes 43 seconds
playing time) at Pasadena,
Calif., in November 1976.

Makaha Beach, Hawaii, provides reputedly the best consistently high waves for surfing, often reaching the rideable limit of 30-35 feet. The highest wave ever ridden was the *tsunami* of "perhaps 50 feet," which struck Minole, Hawaii, on April 3, 1868, and was ridden to save his life by a Hawaiian named Holua.

Competitive swimming originated in London *c.* 1837, at which time there were five or more pools in England, the earliest of which had been opened at St. George's Pier Head, Liverpool, in 1828.

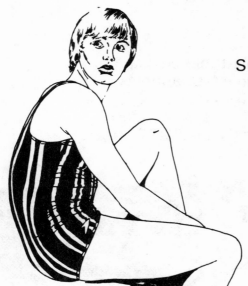

Super-star swimmer Shane Gould of Australia, before she was 16 years old, broke every free-style record from 100 to 1,500 meters.

GUINNESS Book of Trivia Records

The "Human Polar Bear," Gustave A. Brickner (b. 1912) went for his daily dip in the Monongahela River of Pennsylvania on January 24, 1963, when the water temperature was 32°F., the air temperature — 18°F., and the wind speed 40 m.p.h. (chill factor — 85°F.). The river was ice-clogged at the time.

The first triple crossing of the English Channel was by Jon Erikson (b. Sept. 6, 1954) (U.S.) in 38 hours 27 minutes, Aug. 11-12, 1981.

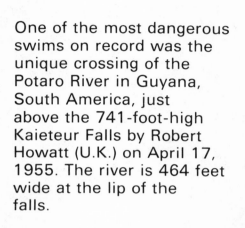

One of the most dangerous swims on record was the unique crossing of the Potaro River in Guyana, South America, just above the 741-foot-high Kaieteur Falls by Robert Howatt (U.K.) on April 17, 1955. The river is 464 feet wide at the lip of the falls.

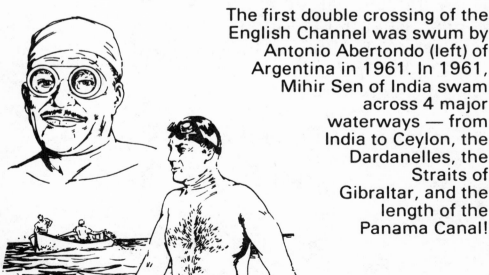

The first double crossing of the English Channel was swum by Antonio Abertondo (left) of Argentina in 1961. In 1961, Mihir Sen of India swam across 4 major waterways — from India to Ceylon, the Dardanelles, the Straits of Gibraltar, and the length of the Panama Canal!

287

The slowest English Channel crossing was the third ever made, when Henry Sullivan (U.S.) swam from England to France in 26 hours 50 min., Aug. 5-6, 1923. It is estimated that he swam 56 miles.

The youngest person ever to swim the English Channel is Markus Hooper (b. June 14, 1967) of Eltham, Kent, England who swam from Dover to Sangatte, France in 14 hours 37 minutes, August 5-6, 1979, when he was 12 years 53 days old.

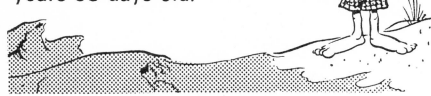

The youngest woman ever to win an Olympic gold medal is Marjorie Gestring (U.S.) (b. November 18, 1922, now Mrs. Bowman) when she was aged 13 years 9 months, in the 1936 women's spring-board event.

Angelica Rozeanu of Rumania holds the Women's Table Tennis Champion title, with 6 World Singles wins (1950, '51, '52, '53, '54, '55).

289

The record number of hits
in 60 seconds in table
tennis is 162 by Nicky Jarvis and Desmond
Douglas in London, England, on December
1, 1976. This was equaled by Douglas and
Paul Day at Blackpool, England, on
March 21, 1977.

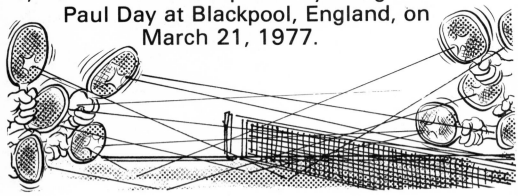

The youngest age at which any
person has won international
honors is 8 years in the case of
Joy Foster, the Jamaican
singles and mixed doubles
table tennis champion in 1958.

In a Swaythling Cup match in Prague on March 14, 1936, between Alex Ehrlich (Poland) and Paneth Farcas (Romania), the opening rally lasted for 1 hour 58 minutes.

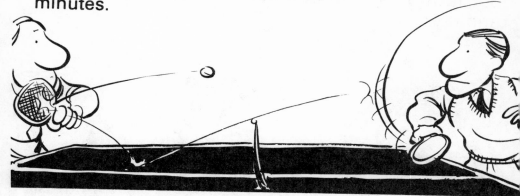

Rick Bowling and Richard De Witt staged a rally lasting 10 hours 9 minutes at the YWCA in New Haven, Conn., on July 26, 1983.

Tennis is the sport with the highest ratio of officials to participants. For a singles match there should be 13 — 10 line, one net-cord and one foot-fault judge, in addition to the umpire.

The youngest tennis champion ever at Wimbledon was Charlotte Dod (1871-1960), who was 15 years 8 months old when she won in 1887.

The fastest tennis serve ever
measured was one of 163.6 m.p.h.
by William Tatem Tilden
(1893-1953) (U.S.) in 1931.

In 1969, before the introduction of the tie-breaker system, Pancho Gonzales (U.S.) played 112 games against Charles Pasarell (U.S.) in the longest match in the history of the Wimbledon championships. In the 5 hour 12 minute match, Gonzales came back from a two-set disadvantage (22-24, 1-6) to take the last three sets (16-14, 6-3, 11-9) and the match.

The tennis career of C. Alphonso Smith (b. 1909) extended from winning the U.S. National Boy's title at Chicago on August 14, 1924, to winning the National 65-and-over title at Aptos, Calif. (exactly 50 years to the day later) on August 14, 1974.

The solo record for trampolining is 240 hours (with 5-min. breaks per hour permissible) by Darlene Blume, at Matraville RSL Youth Club, NSW, Australia, May 8-18, 1980.

Al Oerter of the U.S. won the discus competition in 4 consecutive Olympic meetings (1956 to 1968), a unique achievement in Olympic track and field.

Robert Neil "Bob" McGuinness (b. 1951) unicycled 3,976 miles across Canada from Halifax to Vancouver in 79 days, June 6-Aug. 24, 1978.

Walter J. Watts set a unicycle duration record when he completed the trans-Canadian leg (4,550 miles) of his round-the-world tour from Vancouver to Halifax in 93 days, May 26 to August 27, 1973.

The longest recorded continuous volleyball marathon is one of 240 hours played by 4 alternating teams of 6 girls from Porta High School, Petersburg, Illinois, from May 31 to June 10, 1974. They played in 8-hour shifts without substitutes or any rest breaks.

Bob L. Schaffer of Suffern, New York, specializes in taking on 6-man volleyball teams single-handedly. His won-lost record since August 16, 1963 is 2,102 wins to only 3 losses.

John Lees, 27, of Brighton, England, Apr. 11- June 3, 1972, walked 2,876 miles across the U.S. from City Hall, Los Angeles, to City Hall, N.Y.C., in 53 days, 12 hours, 15 min. (53.746 miles per day).

The longest recorded hike is
one of 18,500 miles through
14 countries from
Singapore to London by
David Kwan, aged 22,
which occupied 81
weeks from May 4, 1957,
or an average of 32 miles
a day.

The longest water polo match on record is one of 67 hours 36 minutes between two teams of 15 from the Townsville Amateur Water Polo Association, Queensland, Australia, on December 1-4, 1978.

The barefoot skiing duration
record is 2 hours 42 minutes
39 seconds by Billy Nichols
on Lake Weir,
Florida, on November
19, 1978.

World championships in water skiing have been
won twice by Alfredo Mendoza (U.S.) in 1953-
55, Mike Suyderhoud (U.S.) in 1967-69, and
George Athans (Canada) in
1971 and 1973.

Jan Suffolk Todd
(U.S.) set the
greatest world
record power
lift for a
woman —
545½ pounds in
a squat, when she
weighed 195 pounds
in June 1981 at
Columbus, Ga.

Between Jan. 24, 1970, and Nov. 1, 1977, Vasili Alexeyev (U.S.S.R.) (b. Jan. 7, 1942) broke a total of 80 official world records in weight lifting.

John "Hercules" Massis of Belgium, on March 19, 1977, raised a weight of 513⅝ pounds to a height of 6 inches from the ground with a bit in his teeth.

The heaviest sportsman of all time was the wrestler William J. Cobb of Macon, Ga., who in 1962 was billed as the 802-lb. ''Happy Humphrey.''

The highest-paid
professional wrestler
is reputedly Lars
Anderson, who
has a $2.3
million 3-year
contract with
the Universal
Wrestling Alliance
in Georgia.

In the latter part of the second millennium B.C., bull leaping was practiced in Crete. Bullfighting in Spain was first reported by the Romans in Baetica (Andalusia) in the third century B.C.

Ron Wyeth of Kingsland, South-
ampton, Hampshire, England,
fished for 336 hours, May 3-16,
1975.

The longest ski jump ever recorded is
one of 181 meters (593 ft. 10 in.) by
Bogdan Norcic (Yugoslavia) (b. 1953),
who fell on landing at
Planica, Yugoslavia,
in Feb. 1977.

A crowd of 40,000
watched a game of polo
played at Jaipur, India,
in 1976, when
elephants were used
instead of ponies.
The length of the
polo sticks used
has not been
ascertained.

Index

316

317